An Introduction to Woodwork

An INTRODUCTION *to* WOODWORK

COLIN HOLCOMBE

The Crowood Press

First published in 2000 by
The Crowood Press Ltd
Ramsbury, Marlborough
Wiltshire SN8 2HR

British Library Cataloguing-in-Publication Data
A catalogue reference for this book is available from the British
Library

ISBN 1 86126 321 X

Illustrations by the author, Simon Williams and Andrew Green.

Dedication
This book is dedicated to my daughters Karen and Susan who
are both making a success of their lives and of whom I am very
proud, and to my late father Ronald Frederick Holcombe who
first encouraged my interest in woodwork.

Acknowledgements
I should like to acknowledge the help of my critic and proof-
reader Jan Hartnell.

By the same author:
How to Restore Antique Furniture
Marquetry Techniques

Typefaces used: New Baskerville (*text*); Optima Bold (*headings*).

Typeset and designed by
D & N Publishing
Membury Business Park, Lambourn Woodlands
Hungerford, Berkshire.

Printed and bound by T.J. International, Padstow.

Contents

Introduction

Why are there so many books on woodwork? One reason is that woodwork is a huge subject, with lots of specialities such as toy making, cabinet making, pattern making, carpentry, turning, veneering, boat-building, marquetry, restoration and carving. No one book can cover all aspects of this varied and interesting subject. It is one of those subjects that can never be known in its entirety by any one man; there is always something new to learn. This book assumes that the reader knows nothing of woodwork and omits nothing essential in its text. Of course, there are things not covered here, pattern making being one, but it will be the only book you require for most aspects of the subject, at least until you find that you want to move on to some more specialist area, such as advanced turning or carving.

The first part examines what tools are available and gives advice on their use and maintenance. This is followed by sections on timber seasoning and storage, some geometry and drawing, methods of fixing with nails, screws and adhesives, and then on to shaping, jointing and construction. There is advice on fitting hinges and other metal components, as well as a section on finishing and polishing. In short, all you need to know to be able to repair or replace woodwork in your home or to make and polish your own furniture. Simply reading this book will not turn you into a craftsman overnight, that will come about only with effort and practice, but it will show you the right way to go and prevent your developing the bad habits that plague so many self-taught woodworkers.

Read the book from cover to cover if you have a mind to, and even if you are an experienced woodworker I would hope that there are things here that will be new to you – you never stop learning. If you have a project in mind that you want to tackle use the index and look up the things that you will need to know as and when you require them. Do you want to know how to sharpen your plane, how to cut a dovetail joint or to fit a hinge? Then look in the appropriate chapter or refer to the index since that is what it is there for.

There was a time, not all that long ago, when woodwork was taught in schools; admittedly this was done in a sexist way, with the girls being largely excluded and marched off for lessons on cooking or sewing. But the boys left school with at least some idea of how to use a saw and a chisel. To learn woodwork properly now, whether you are male or female, you can go to a night school or a technical college, or you can teach yourself with the aid of a good book, possibly even this one.

I had the advantage of a good woodwork teacher at school, a father with an interest in woodwork and a well-equipped workshop. I have done my best over the years to pass on some of the things I have learnt to those who want to know; at first this was by teaching furniture restoration and polishing at an adult night school for some twenty years and now with this book that I hope you will find interesting as well as useful.

I learnt the fundamentals of woodwork at Bishop Road Secondary Modern School in Bristol, under the watchful eye of Mr Hody. After leaving school I started an apprenticeship with a firm of antique dealers, as a restorer of antique furniture. Most of what I know about cabinet making was learnt at this time from an Italian restorer by the name of Carlo Perona. Carlo was a wonderful craftsman with a huge knowledge of life as well as of all things to do with wood, and I regret to this day not making notes or recordings of any of his many anecdotes. But one I do remember concerned a time when Carlo was working in a large workshop in his home town of San Remo. Several men were in the veneer shop, working with quite large sheets and putting them down with hot Scotch glue. You can picture the scene, with these men busily working away, each with his own pot of glue, and working fast so that the work would not become cold before they were finished. The head of the company chooses this time to bring a customer into the workshop to inspect the work in progress. The customer turned out to be a very rich client, a lady in a fur coat with a small, long-haired and very yappy dog on a long lead. The boss and the client stopped for a chat quite close to Carlo's bench and the dog was making a nuisance of itself at Carlo's feet. After putting up with this and the indifference of the owner for a while, Carlo eventually politely asked whether the dog could be kept away, because it was interfering with the work in progress. The rich, arrogant owner, who obviously did not wish to be addressed by a common workman, treated this request with some contempt and the boss, who was annoyed at having his conversation interrupted, simply glared. Needless to say, the conversation continued in the same spot and the dog continued fussing about at Carlo's feet. The next time Carlo picked up a fully-loaded glue brush it was unfortunately wiped along the full length of the over-excited dog's back, a fact that was not discovered until the lady was about to leave and invited the animal to leap into her arms. It apparently took copious amounts of water to separate fur coat and dog, and everybody took Carlo's assurances that it had been an unfortunate accident with a pinch of salt.

Many of Carlo's anecdotes were made believable by his occasional outrageous behaviour and his obvious disregard for health and safety. One day, early on in my apprenticeship, I was sent up a tall pair of steps, with a dustpan and brush, to clean the tops of the metal hoods that covered the fluorescent lights in the workshop. After a few moments of watching me struggle to collect the sawdust in the pan, without covering the people below or falling off the steps, Carlo beckoned me down. He said that he had a much better and quicker way to achieve the same result. In the workshop at that time we had one or two aerosol cans of gold paint that were mostly now too nearly empty to be of further use. Carlo selected one of these cans and, dragging me after him by the sleeve, proceeded to place one on the gas ring and light up. We then rather quickly got hold of the other person who was working there at the time and left the room. The three of us stood outside the door until there was a mighty bang from inside. When we once again entered the room we were greeted by great clouds of dust, descending from on high; it was as just as if it was snowing sawdust. 'There', declared Carlo proudly, 'I tell you is a quicker these way, no?' I had to admit that the light hoods were now much less dusty; but from then on everyone seemed to want to leave the room in a hurry whenever Carlo went anywhere near the gas ring.

THE WORKSHOP

Most people who work in wood at home have a corner in the garage that they use rather than an actual workshop. This is probably all well and good in the summer, but garages are difficult to heat and to draught-proof, which makes polishing impossible in the winter and any fine woodwork a chore rather than a pleasure. So if it is the garage that you intend to use there are a few things that will have to be attended to. To start with, unless you intend to give up any woodworking activity throughout the winter you will need some form of heating, and whatever kind you choose it will not be very efficient unless the garage door can be draught-proofed in some way. The cheapest and easiest form of draught-proofing is simply to hang a heavy curtain across the inside of the door. While on the subject of heating, it must be remembered that naked flames are not a good idea in a dusty environment or in one where there are inflammable liquids. Oil-filled radiators or night-storage heaters are the safest means, whereas gas fires are a definite hazard. If it is at all possible, a spare or box room in the house will make a much more comfortable workshop than the garage, although, of course, this does have the disadvantage of interfering more with the rest of the household. A curtain placed against the inside of the door will help to prevent sawdust from filtering through to the rest of the house; however, machinery is probably best left in the garage, even if it is fitted with a dust bag.

If you are setting up a workshop for the first time one of the first things you will require is a suitable bench. You can buy one ready made, of course, but most serious woodworkers will want to make one to suit their own specific needs. When designing a bench much consideration must be given to its height, and the best height will be different for different people. Stand at a table and go through the motions of planing or sawing a piece of wood. You have to be able to stand over and work on the wood without stooping too much, a great deal of back trouble may be avoided by not having too low a working height. Make the bench a little higher than you think necessary; it can always be

cut down a little subsequently. The overall dimensions of the bench will depend upon the available space in the room: a large bench is good, but only if it does not restrict the usable space in the workshop. The bench will need at least six legs and they will have to be quite sturdy. Pine or beech, or both, is fine for the material and it is not necessary to have a tool well if you do not want one. I do, however, recommend a drawer for small tools, pencils and the like. The peg front, as shown overleaf, enables larger items to be supported while they are in the vice. This is especially helpful with things such as drawer fronts and table tops. Waxing the bench will help to prevent glue from sticking to the surfaces and will keep the bench clean. It is important to keep the bench clean because bits of dried glue and the like may easily mark a piece of wood placed on it; this may result in extra cleaning-up and sanding, or even ruin a piece of veneered work.

I recommend that you fit as large a vice as the bench size and your pocket will allow, even if you intend only ever working on small items; a large vice is more versatile and will hold items more securely. A bench stop for planing against should be fitted at one end of the bench; there are several different types on the market. The peg front that I recommend is a series of holes in the centre leg of the bench into which a large peg or support may be placed at different heights to help in holding larger items, such as table tops, only one end of which could be in the vice at a time.

If you work mostly in the workshop itself rather than on site somewhere tools can be kept in racks behind the bench rather than in tool chests or boxes. This means that when a specific tool is required it can easily be selected and replaced from behind the bench rather than have to be searched for in a toolbox. One of the best ways of storing tools so that they are easily accessible is to fix a length of wood to the wall behind the

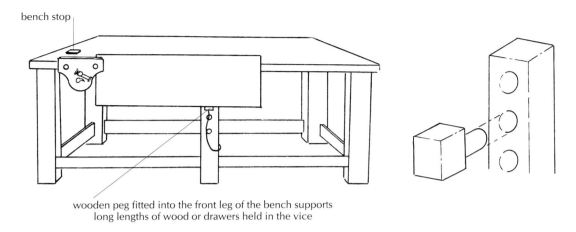

bench stop

wooden peg fitted into the front leg of the bench supports
long lengths of wood or drawers held in the vice

Bench with peg front for supporting table tops and the like.

bench and to nail a length of old electric cable to it. The cable is nailed in such a way as to make a series of differently sized loops into which the tools can be slotted.

The setting out of the workshop will need some consideration. Do not place machinery where it will be in the way when not in use, but ensure that there is enough space for the wood to be worked on and passed through it. It is no good placing a band saw or circular saw facing a wall where the length of wood that can be passed through would be severely restricted. Such equipment should be placed along the wall with an adequate space in front and behind the work-table to accommodate a reasonable length of wood. The bench will need to be in a well-lit location and some standing area will be necessary for the cabinet or item you are working on.

You will need somewhere to store timber and it may be best to store it in the garage or garden shed or even under a tarpaulin in the garden. Lengths of timber must be stored flat and be supported at regular intervals along their length. See the section on seasoning in Chapter 7 for more information on stacking timber. If the timber has to be stored in the workshop itself make some sturdy racking to keep it flat and out of the way. This may usually be done by making some racking that is suspended from the ceiling rafters.

Cables in a workshop may be a hazard and so make sure that you have plenty of power points in order to escape the need to drape cables across the room. The secret of avoiding accidents is to be tidy, to put things away when they are not in use, and to have a place for everything and keep everything in its place. Polishes and any other inflammable liquids are best kept in a metal bin of some kind; a metal dustbin is ideal for this purpose. Ventilation may be a consideration if you are going to be using paint strippers or impact adhesives so it is worth considering the installation of an extractor fan.

— **1** —

Tools for Measuring and Marking

THE RULE

The most common rule now in use is the tape rule. It is found in every tool bag and workshop or garage in the country. Tape rules may be purchased in a multitude of different lengths, widths and qualities. Choose the rule that best suits your individual needs; if you are going to be doing a lot of building work or house carpentry you may need a rule that extends further than if you were only ever doing picture framing or cabinet making. If you are regularly taking room measurements on your own you will find it helpful to have a rule with a wide, stiff tape that can be extended some distance without collapsing.

But whichever rule you choose make sure that it is a quality rule with clear markings that are easily read. The biggest drawback to this type of rule is the fact that the end has a hooked piece of metal, designed so that it can be butted against a surface or hooked over an edge. This end piece is fitted in such a way as to compensate for its own thickness. This may be a disadvantage when doing bench work because it is more accurate when measuring between pencil marks not to start from the end of the rule and this may cause confusion.

For bench work it is better to use a stiff wooden or steel rule. Steel rules may be purchased in sizes from 150mm to 1m. Wooden rules may be purchased in similar

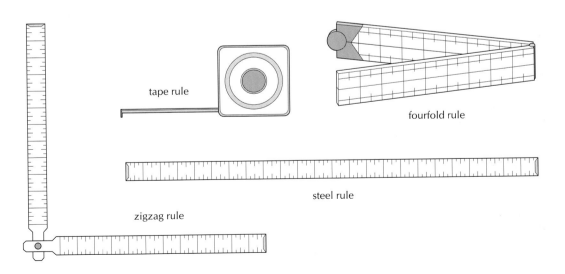

The most common types of rule.

sizes to those made of steel, but also come in a folding form, in either the old fourfold or the zigzag type.

THE STRAIGHTEDGE

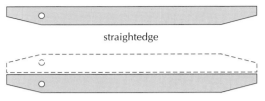

Straightedges can be in wood or metal.

Straightedges may be bought in either steel or wood and of varying sizes, or you can make your own. They are used for testing the flatness of surfaces or for drawing straight lines. To test a straightedge for accuracy place it on a flat surface and draw a line along its full length, then turn the straightedge over and compare the edge with the line just drawn. If they coincide then the straightedge is accurate.

PINCH RODS

Pinch rods are simply two rules, lengths of dowel or laths held together by hand at the centre and extended out until they reach the sides of an opening. They are used when checking the distance between the walls of an alcove at particular heights. Pinch rods may also be used to check the squareness of a frame by comparing the lengths of its diagonals.

TRY-SQUARE

The basic and most commonly used square in woodwork is the classic try-square with a steel blade and wooden stock. To check that the square is accurate place the stock against a prepared straight edge and draw a line the full length of the blade. Turn the square over and try the edge against the line just drawn: if they correspond then the square is true.

Whenever using a square of this type to mark the end of a piece of wood or the shoulders of a joint always remember that 'stock and faces go together'. That is to say, that the stock of the square should only ever be placed against either the face side or the face edge of a piece of work.

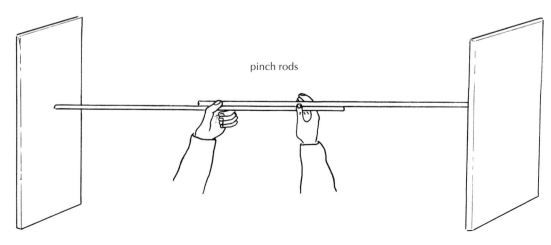

Measuring an internal diameter with pinch rods.

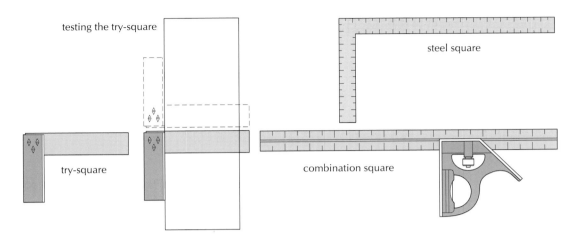

Various types of woodworking square.

When testing to see whether a piece of wood is square it is best to hold the square in position and sight along the work facing the light; in this way even a small discrepancy will be obvious. Remember to slide the square along the work or to test at several points along its length, not just in one place.

COMBINATION SQUARE

This is a multi-purpose square that can be used as an inside or an outside try square, mitre square and also as a depth gauge. This square has an adjustable head that is also fitted with a spirit level for horizontal and plumb readings.

STEEL SQUARE

The steel square is another type that is very useful; it may be used for checking the squareness of larger items and, because it does not have a stock, it can be laid flat which makes it invaluable in marking out.

THE BEVEL

The bevel is used for checking and marking angles that are not right angles. The common bevel has a wooden or metal stock with a slot into which the blade may be folded when it is not in use. Its blade is slotted so that its angle and length can be adjusted. When setting the desired angle it is often found that the action of tightening the screw or wing nut on the bevel will slightly

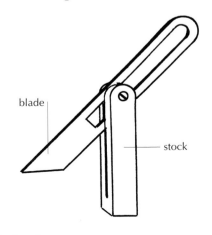

The bevel.

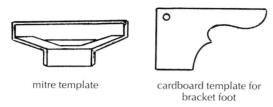

mitre template   cardboard template for
                           bracket foot

Marking templates.

alter the set angle. It is thus best to check the angle again and, if adjustment is needed, to tap the blade lightly on the bench to adjust and then retighten the screw.

TEMPLATE

A template may be either a pattern cut out in paper, card, plywood or some other material that is used to draw out several similarly shaped pieces, or it may be a tool-guiding appliance for cutting angles, as with a mitre template which can be used, for example, for paring the mitres on glazing bars.

GAUGES

MARKING GAUGE

The ordinary marking gauge has only one point and is used for marking lines parallel to the edge of the work. The pin that actually does the marking is at one end of a wooden stem, which in turn passes through a head or stock. The stem is tightened by means of a thumbscrew. To adjust it the thumbscrew is loosened and the stem adjusted to the correct distance after which the screw is retightened. For fine adjustment either end of the stem may be tapped on the bench. The gauge comes with a flat stock, to be used against a straight edge, but by cutting a dowel rod in half and pinning

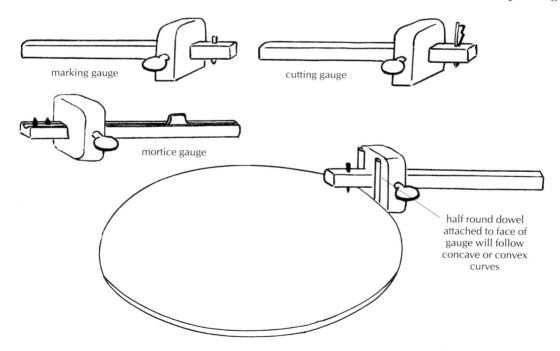

marking gauge

cutting gauge

mortice gauge

half round dowel
attached to face of
gauge will follow
concave or convex
curves

Marking gauges.

or gluing the two halves to the face of the stock as shown the gauge can also be used to follow a concave or convex edge.

MORTISE GAUGE

The mortise gauge is the same as a marking gauge except that it has a second, independently adjustable pin. The gauge is used, as the name implies, for marking mortise and tenon joints. To set the gauge, first adjust as a marking gauge so that the fixed pin is positioned to mark the far side of the mortise and then adjust the second pin in position. Another method of setting is to set the position of the two pins so that they are the correct distance apart and then to adjust the position of the gauge stock against the side of the work.

CUTTING GAUGE

The cutting gauge differs from the marking gauge only inasmuch as it has a small cutting blade rather than a pin. This makes it especially suitable for marking out inlays and rebates.

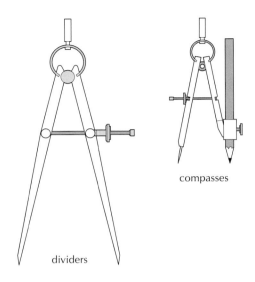

compasses

dividers

Compasses and dividers.

COMPASSES AND DIVIDERS

Compasses and dividers are primarily used in the drawing and marking-out stages of

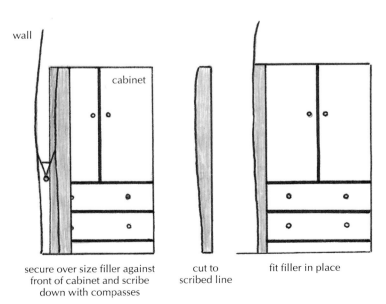

secure over size filler against front of cabinet and scribe down with compasses

cut to scribed line

fit filler in place

Scribing in a filler strip.

15

some items, but they are also used for scribing in. For example, if you are fitting a filler panel between a wall and a built-in cabinet such as a wardrobe, as shown on the previous page, it is unlikely that the wall will be either upright or even and a method of accurately marking that side of the filler will be needed. The cabinet is positioned and fixed in place, after which the filler panel is positioned temporarily in front of the cabinet, touching the wall, upright and at the correct height. The filler panel will be touching the wall at some points but at others there will be a gap. The compasses are opened to the width of the largest gap. Now, with one side of the compasses held lightly against the wall, a line is scribed down the front of the panel that will exactly follow the undulations of the wall, just over the distance between the filler panel and the wall at the widest point. When the filler panel is cut to the line it will fit exactly to the wall and all that remains to be done is to mark the width of the panel required at the top and the bottom of the cabinet and to cut a straight line between these two points.

TRAMMEL HEADS

These are used for marking out larger diameters, such as circular table tops, that cannot be handled by ordinary compasses. They may be attached to the ends of a piece of wood; this may be of any length.

Trammel heads.

CALLIPERS

Standard callipers are a little like dividers. They are used for measuring either internal or external diameters and can be purchased in a variety of sizes, some with a screw assembly for fine adjustment.

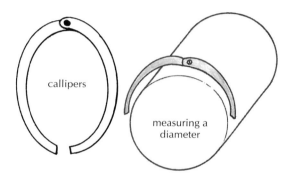

callipers

measuring a diameter

Diameters are measured with callipers.

SLIDE CALLIPERS

These are used for measuring the thickness of wood and small diameters and lengths; they may also be used, for instance, to check the depth of dowel holes.

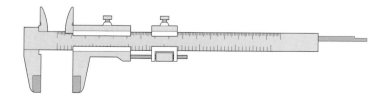

Slide callipers.

— 2 —

Saws and Sawing

THE CROSSCUT SAW

As the name suggests, this saw is used for cutting wood across the grain and it generally has seven or eight teeth to the inch. As with other saws, the teeth are bent to the side, alternating left and right. This bending of the teeth is called the 'set' and is done so that the groove cut by the saw is wider than the blade in order to prevent the blade from binding. The teeth are sharpened at an angle so as to present a point to the timber rather than an edge, making cutting far smoother and easier. The amount of set required will depend upon the type of wood being cut. Softwoods require a greater amount of set than hardwoods and wet timber requires more than dry.

One aspect of sawing which the novice sometimes finds difficult is actually getting started. The best way to start a cut is to position a thumb nail against the mark on the wood, place the saw against the nail and draw the saw back once or twice to get started. Do not push the saw forward to start as there is a danger that the blade will jump and damage either the work or the user. The two most common mistakes made when using saws, not just by the beginner but also by those with some experience, is to push the saw too hard and not use the full length of the blade. When sawing, the blade should be pulled back lightly and then pushed forward in a long stroke allowing the saw's own weight to do the work; in this way an accurate cut may be obtained. Push too hard and the saw will deviate off line, forcing the user to try to correct his cut and to bend the blade. Take care at the end of a cut to slow down the stroke a little and to make sure that the waste part of the wood is supported, otherwise it will fall off before the cut is complete, causing splintering along the grain.

THE RIPSAW

The ripsaw is designed to cut timber along the grain, and usually has four teeth to the inch. It is used in the same manner as the crosscut saw. However, it is not much used now as most woodworkers have access to some form of machinery that will do the job quickly and accurately.

THE PANEL SAW

This is now the most commonly used handsaw since it can be employed for both ripping with the grain and crosscutting. It will not cut with the grain as fast as a ripsaw but it is very versatile and will cope with most of the tasks asked of it. The panel saw is a good alternative to owning both a ripsaw and a crosscut saw.

Top view of teeth filed and set.

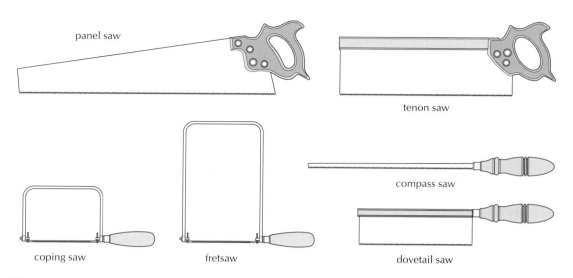

The most common woodworking saws.

THE TENON SAW

Chiefly used for bench work and the cutting of joints, this saw has a brass or steel back along the top edge of the blade that gives it strength and rigidity, thus enabling a greater accuracy in sawing. The tenon saw is often used in conjunction with the bench hook.

THE BENCH HOOK

The bench hook is made by attaching a batten to each side of a flat piece of wood. The bottom batten hooks over the front of the bench and the top one acts as a stop against which is held the piece of wood being cut.

THE DOVETAIL SAW

The dovetail saw is really no more than a small tenon saw with fine teeth. It is used for cutting dovetails or any other fine work.

BOW SAWS AND COPING SAWS

Both these saws are designed for cutting out patterns in wood. Outside curved lines are easily followed with these saws and closed patterns can also be cut; the latter is done by detaching one end of the blade and passing it through a hole drilled in the waste part of the pattern before reattaching the blade end for cutting.

THE FRETSAW

The fretsaw is a specialist tool used in a similar way to the coping saw but intended for the cutting of delicate fretwork or in the making of marquetry. The fretsaw is used in conjunction with a wooden platform, often referred to as a bird's mouth because of the vee-shaped cut-out through which the blade passes. In use, the fretsaw is moved up and down and the work being cut is moved on to the blade.

THE COMPASS, PAD OR KEYHOLE SAW

Compass saws are used for cutting closed patterns in timber where a bow or coping saw will not reach. These saws may be purchased with a detachable handle called a 'pad', which allows for a variety of blades to be fitted and is the reason these saws are sometimes referred to as pad saws. Such saws have now been largely superseded by the powered jigsaw.

SETTING AND SHARPENING

The equipment needed to set and sharpen a saw is a triangular saw file, of the correct size for the saw, a saw set and some device for holding the blade along its full length in the vice. Two long battens, cut to fit around the handle of the saw, are usually employed for this purpose. The battens are placed on either side of the blade to hold the blade straight. The ordinary bench vice may be used for setting and sharpening but it is a little low for comfort. However, a stand can be made as shown, called a 'saw chops', which has tapered slots at the top into which the strips of batten are fitted and gently tapped into place so that the whole structure is securely held.

SETTING THE TEETH

Saw teeth are given a set to ensure that the groove or 'kerf' that the saw cuts is wider than the blade in order to prevent it from binding in the wood, as described earlier in this chapter.

The saw may or may not need setting; if it cuts a wide kerf then it will not need to be set. The setting can be done after the saw is sharpened, but it is more usual to do it first. Saw teeth can be set with either a notched saw set, in which case the amount of set will have to be judged each time, or preferably a pliers-type of saw set with a plunger may be used. The pliers-type can be adjusted for different sizes of teeth by turning a revolving disc, and this is by far

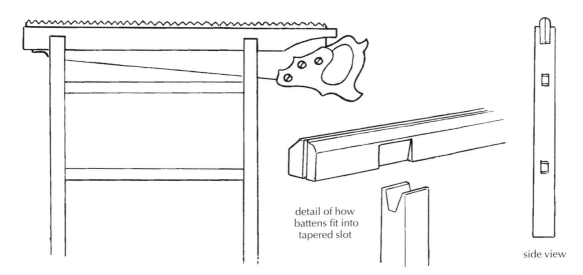

detail of how battens fit into tapered slot

side view

The saw chops.

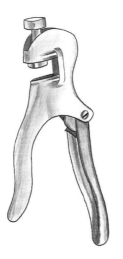

Saw set.

none of them are standing up proud of the rest. Do not remove much metal because this operation is intended simply to make sure that the teeth are all level and to put a 'shiner', an area of bright, newly-filed metal, on the tips of all the teeth. To sharpen, start from the handle end of the saw on the face of the first tooth bent away from you. For ripsaws, hold the file horizontal in the gullet to get the angle of tilt of the file, and file across at right angles to the blade, removing half the shiner produced when topping. Repeat in alternate gullets to the end of the blade, then reverse the saw and file the remaining gullets, removing the other half of the shiner. Try to establish a steady rhythm as this will help to ensure that you use the same pressure on each tooth filed. Some woodworkers will say that the file should point slightly towards the handle during sharpening, and there is no harm in this, indeed, with timber that does not have a very straight grain it may be beneficial. For crosscut saws the procedure is the same as for ripsaws, except that, after topping, the file is placed in the first gullet at an angle of 65 to 70 degrees, pointing towards the handle, rather than at right angles. File the alternate gullets, turn the saw and repeat with the other teeth.

the best method to use. Go along the side of the blade and set every other tooth, turn the saw around and repeat on the other side, setting the remaining teeth.

SHARPENING

The first step is to 'top' the blade by attaching the battens and placing it in the vice, teeth up. Lightly run a flat, fine file along the top of the teeth to ensure that

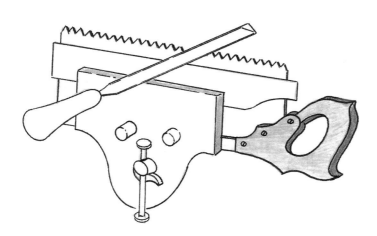

A tenon saw can often be sharpened in the vice.

Hammers, Chisels and Gouges

HAMMERS AND MALLETS

The three most common hammers in use today are the Warrington hammer, the London hammer and the claw hammer, as shown. Their heads are made of cast steel and are slightly convex, so that the surface of the wood is not so easily marked if it is hit accidentally. The thin end of the hammerhead is known as the 'pene', and these hammers are often referred to as pene hammers in order to differentiate between them and claw hammers. The pene is useful for starting off small nails

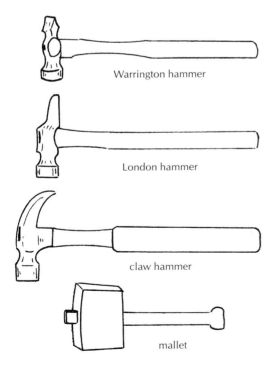

Warrington hammer

London hammer

claw hammer

mallet

Various types of hammer.

held between the finger and the thumb or for driving nails into grooves or other restricted places. The handle, or shaft, of the hammer is made of ash or beech, ash being the better of the two because it is more able to withstand the sudden jars of hammering. The handle is fitted through the head and is secured by a wedge of wood or steel driven into the end. The slot cut to receive the wedge is best cut across the head as this is the direction in which the head will tend to work loose. Claw hammers are most often used by carpenters and are useful for pulling out nails as well driving them in.

A mallet may best be described as a wooden hammer and is used in those circumstances where a hammer would cause damage, such as when hammering the end of a chisel when mortising. Mallets are usually made of beech and the hole in the head through which the handle passes is tapered so that the action of using the mallet will tend to tighten rather than loosen it.

CHISELS AND GOUGES

There are three basic types of chisel for general woodwork: the firmer chisel, the paring chisel and the mortise chisel. The firmer, general-purpose chisel is thicker than the paring chisel and is usually square-sided. The paring chisel, which is used for taking fine shavings of wood when shaping, is bevel-sided. These two chisels traditionally had wooden handles, but now more commonly have high-impact plastic handles, which allow them to be struck without splintering.

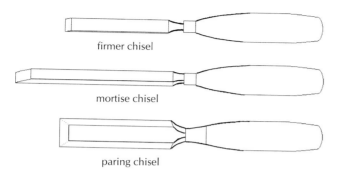

firmer chisel

mortise chisel

paring chisel

The most common chisels.

FIRMER AND PARING CHISELS

When chiselling a slot in a piece of wood the side of the slot will first have to be cut with a tenon saw. The slot is then chiselled out a little at a time, working first from one side and then from the other. If the slot were chiselled out entirely from one side there would be a chance that the edge on the far side would splinter off. When paring wood in the direction of the length of the timber it is important to do so in the direction of the grain otherwise there is a risk of the chisel's digging in and splitting the wood. When paring the corner of a piece of wood always work towards the end and not the side to prevent splintering, and with all work involving chisels remember that it is best to take a little at a time and not try to complete the task in one go.

MORTISE CHISEL

The mortise chisel is stronger than the firmer chisel, being thicker in the blade in order to be able to take some leverage. When cutting a mortise make sure that the wood is held securely, either in a vice or, preferably, cramped to the bench. Hold the mortise chisel upright and stand in line with it for sighting rather than to one side. Start in the middle of the mortise and give the chisel a firm blow with the mallet, driving it into the wood. Push the handle of the chisel away from you, keeping it in an upright position; this will release the chisel so that it can be withdrawn. Position the chisel once again, but this time a little nearer to you and repeat the action. This time, when you push the chisel away from you, not only will you release it so that it can be withdrawn, but the action will also break away a section of timber and pulling the chisel backwards will lift this clear of the joint. Continue in this way until you almost reach the line marking the end of the mortise, but do not go right up to it. Turn the chisel around, go back to the

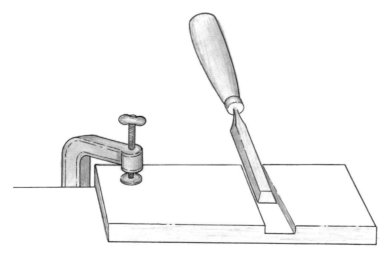

Work from one side and then the other.

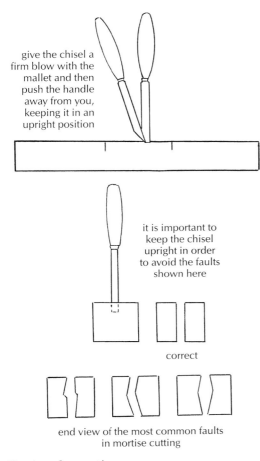

give the chisel a firm blow with the mallet and then push the handle away from you, keeping it in an upright position

it is important to keep the chisel upright in order to avoid the faults shown here

correct

end view of the most common faults in mortise cutting

Cutting the mortise.

centre of the joint and repeat the procedure in the opposite direction, once again going almost up to the line marking the end of the mortise. Check its depth and repeat the operation until the desired depth has been reached. If a through mortise is required the work must be turned over and the procedure repeated on the other side of the wood until the chisel breaks through. When this happens or when the correct depth has been reached the ends of the joint may be cleaned down, up to the line. This time do not lever the chisel back against the edge of the joint because this will damage the edge and it is possible that this will show after the joint has been assembled.

GOUGES

A gouge will be one of two types: the inside-ground paring gouge and the outside-ground firmer gouge. Gouges come in a variety of widths and curves and are used for such jobs as scribing internal curves, as on the end of a chair rail (paring gouge), or for cutting finger grips (firmer gouge).

CARVING GOUGES

Carving chisels and gouges differ from firmer and paring gouges in that they are sharpened with bevels on both sides. The outer bevel is of the order of 15 degrees and is obtained by sharpening on a flat oil-stone. The chisel is held at the correct angle, while being pushed backwards and forwards on the stone and simultaneously twisted so that every part of the bevel is honed. The inner bevel is honed with a special sharpening stone (a slip stone) of the appropriate dimensions and is usually about one-quarter of the length of the outer bevel but with the same angle. The use of slip is described in Chapter 5.

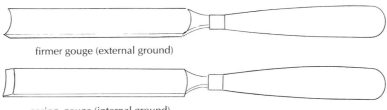

firmer gouge (external ground)

paring gouge (internal ground)

Gouges.

23

Tools for Boring

THE BRADAWL

Small holes that do not go deep into the wood, such as those for starting a screw in softwood or for marking a place to be drilled so as to give the drill a start and stop it from wandering, can be bored with a bradawl. The end of the bradawl is filed to an edge like a chisel rather than to a point; a pointed bradawl is merely a pricker, it cannot bore. In use, the sharpened end of the bradawl is held across the grain and pressed into the timber. While being pressed the bradawl is rotated back and forth. Sometimes it is driven into the wood with a blow from a hammer but even then the cutting edge must be across and not in line with the grain, and the bradawl should be rotated before it is withdrawn otherwise withdrawal may be difficult.

THE GIMLET

The gimlet is a self-contained boring tool like a bradawl, but with a twisted point that forces its way into the wood. The gimlet has only limited application and is little used today.

THE WHEEL BRACE

The wheel brace or hand drill will accept most twist drills up to 8mm and can reach some places where an electric drill would be difficult to use.

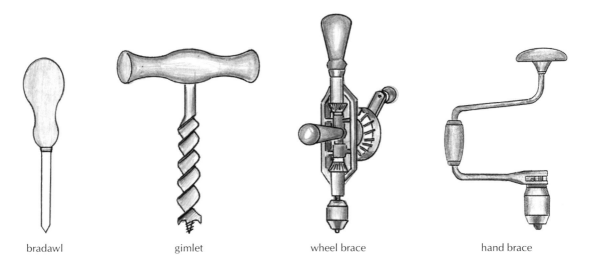

| bradawl | gimlet | wheel brace | hand brace |

Tools for boring.

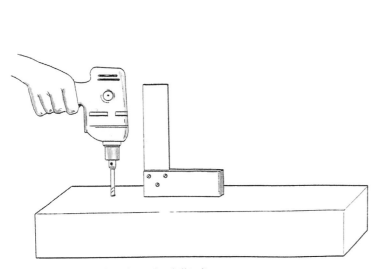

a square will help to keep the drill in line

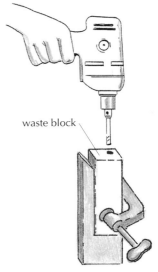

waste block

a shaped block will help to stop the drill wandering off line when drilling mitres

Most drilling is now done with an electric drill.

THE HAND BRACE

Larger holes are best drilled with a hand brace, which is really a cranked shaft, revolving a chuck. Most braces have a ratchet mechanism to allow them to be used in a confined space.

GENERAL OBSERVATIONS ON DRILLING

Nearly all drilling now is done with an electric drill and this is hardly surprising; the electric drill is fast and with a sharp bit in place will drill the hardest of timbers with ease. Accuracy, however, is still something that is best achieved with a hand or wheel brace, unless a pillar drill is available.

When drilling a hole which needs to be at right angles to the surface of the wood first make sure that the piece in question is upright in the vice or flat on the bench. A set square may be positioned as a guide, and it is best to stand back from the work as far as is practicable, rather than to stand over it. View the work from one angle and drill a little, then view from a different angle and drill some more. Sometimes it is possible to put a dowel into the hole just started and then to place a set square on the surface of the work and up against it to check for accuracy.

When there is a need to start a hole on a surface that is not flat, such as a mitre, a block of waste wood may be cut and cramped in place to start things off.

When drilling right through a piece of wood there is a real possibility that the drill will splinter the wood on the far side as it emerges. This may be avoided by cramping a piece of waste wood in place over the spot where the drill will come through. When using a centre or twist bit in a hand brace it is possible to drill until just the point emerges on the far side and then withdraw the bit, turn the work over and finish drilling from the reverse side without causing any damage.

THE DRILL BITS

For drilling small holes in wood the ordinary carbon steel or high-speed metal drill will do the job, but the wood drill or brad point is specially designed for drilling wood and is a far better option. Both of these bits can be held in either a wheel brace or an electric drill. Larger holes are drilled with either a twist bit, a centre bit or a spade bit, the first two being held in a hand brace and the last in an electric drill. There are other tools, such as expanding bits and hole cutters, that are available for even larger holes.

The drill bits most commonly used in conjunction with the hand brace are twist bits of which there are two patterns. The solid centre or single spiral bit with only one twist and the Jennings pattern that has a double twist. Both of these have a screw end that draws the bit into the wood and cutters on the circumference that scribe out the hole. Other bits that may be used are the centre bit, used for drilling shallow holes, and the Forstner bit that has no end screw and is useful for drilling holes where a flat bottom is required.

Countersink bits, for letting in the heads of screws, can be purchased to fit electric drills or hand braces, and now it is even possible to buy combination bits that both drill the screw hole and countersink in the one action.

Forstner bit

twist bit

centre bit

metal bit

Various drill bits.

Tools for Sharpening and Grinding

No cutting tool is of any real use unless it is sharp. Knowing how to maintain and sharpen your tools is as important as knowing the correct way to use them. Plane irons and chisels have a grinding bevel and a sharpening bevel. The grinding angle is usually 25 degrees and the sharpening angle 30 degrees; however, many chisels when purchased new will have only the grinding bevel and will need to be sharpened before they can be used.

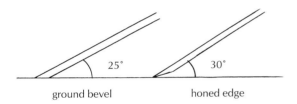

Grinding and sharpening angles.

GRINDING

There are two types of grindstone readily available to the woodworker: the dry-stone bench grinder and the wet-stone grinder. The first is the cheaper option but has the drawback of a fast speed making it very easy to overheat the iron or chisel being sharpened. The wet-stone grinder is generally more expensive, but with a wet wheel and a slower speed the danger of overheating is more or less eliminated.

The iron to be sharpened has to be held against the wheel at an angle of 25 degrees. This is usually done by holding it manually; but this calls for some practice and many grindstones now have tool rests that make the task much easier. Care must be taken to

bench grinder

the blade will need to be cooled in water if it becomes hot during grinding

ALWAYS WEAR SAFETY GOGGLES

wet-stone grinders prevent loss of temper caused by overheating and reduce the risk of accidents associated with high speed grinders

Dry and wet stone grinders.

ensure that the blade does not become too hot as this will affect the temper of the blade and cause it to lose its edge more quickly. If the blade is overheating it will start to discolour and go blue, thus contact with the stone should be stopped at the first sign of this happening and the blade allowed to cool. Always remember to wear safety glasses or goggles when using a grindstone.

SHARPENING

Oilstones for sharpening come in several qualities; some are natural stones and some are man-made combination stones with a coarse or medium side and a fine finishing side. An alternative to oilstones is either a Japanese water-stone or a ceramic whetstone. Japanese water-stones are softer than oilstones and are easily damaged, but they are well worth their extra cost and effort for the finish they give. Ceramic stones are extremely hard and efficient

sharpening stones, employing synthetic sapphires. They are used completely dry and leave a highly polished finish on the sharpened blade without the mess associated with a wet system.

The sharpening of chisels and plane irons is done in the same way and so the following description may be applied to both. For a right-handed person the right hand is chiefly used to push the blade forwards and backwards and the left one is used to press the edge on to the stone. The blade is presented to the stone at an angle of about 30 degrees but it must be a comfortable angle for you to maintain. The lower the blade is held the more metal has to be removed but the finer and better the cutting edge will be. The blade must be kept at a constant angle with any up and down movement avoided (the main fault of the beginner). The blade is moved over the surface of the stone in either a straight up and down or a circular movement until a slight burr is detected on the reverse side

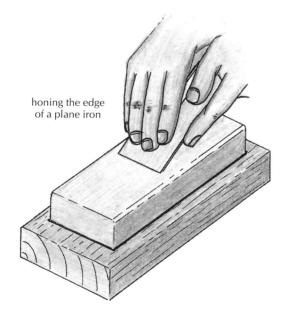

honing the edge
of a plane iron

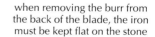

when removing the burr from
the back of the blade, the iron
must be kept flat on the stone

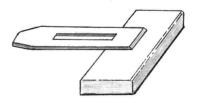

Using the oil stone.

The slip stone in use.

inside ground gouge being
sharpened with a slip stone

outside ground gouge will have
the burr removed in this way

of the blade (the flat side). This burr has to be removed by turning the blade over and holding it completely flat on the stone and rubbing it backwards and forwards a few times. The blade is then checked for sharpness. This is usually done by drawing the thumb across the edge; however, this is not really necessary as it is possible to see whether the blade is sharp by simply looking at it. A fine white line on the edge of the blade betrays that it is dull. If the edge cannot be seen then it is sharp. The presence or not of the white line is best observed by tilting the edge backwards and forwards to catch the light. If the blade is still dull then the process must be repeated.

SLIP STONES

Slip stones are small oilstones, tapered in section and with curved edges. They are used for sharpening gouges and carving chisels. A gouge that is ground on the outside may, of course, be sharpened on an ordinary oilstone, by rubbing it backwards and forwards just as with an ordinary chisel but rotating it at the same time. For coarse work it is not necessary to remove the burr, but for fine work the burr is removed with a slip stone, taking great care not to put a bevel on the reverse side. Gouges that are ground on the inside will have to be sharpened with the slip stone, and then have the burr removed on an ordinary oilstone. The constant sharpening of gouges and even of small chisels on a flat oilstone will eventually cause it to become hollow in the centre, rendering it unsuitable for sharpening plane irons. For this reason it is always a good idea to keep an old stone specifically for such jobs.

HONING GUIDES

Honing guides may be purchased to hold the blade at any chosen angle when placed on the stone. These are well worth trying out if you are unsure of your ability to hold the blade at a constant angle.

— 6 —

The Plane

THE WOODEN PLANE

There are three basic sizes of the standard bench plane: the try plane, the jack plane and the smoothing plane. They come with either a wooden or a metal body, but today the metal body is by far the more popular and is easily available. However, a brief description of the wooden plane may be of interest.

The wooden plane remained popular far longer on the continent than in this country, as many woodworkers prefer the easy way in which the wooden plane slips over the surface of the work. The plane blade is held in place with a wooden wedge and there are two ways by which to release it: the first is to turn the plane over, hold the iron and wedge in one hand and tap the front of the plane smartly on the edge of the bench. The second method is to tap the front of the plane with a hammer to loosen the wedge. The adjusting of the blade is carried out by tapping the front of the plane, as just described,

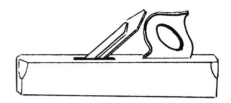

Wooden smoothing plane.

to loosen the wedge and then tapping the end of the blade to lower it and increase the thickness of the cut. Once the desired depth of cut has been obtained the wedge is tapped down to hold the blade firmly in place. The body of the plane is made of beech and should be oiled to maintain a smooth 'slip' over the surface of the work.

THE METAL PLANE

The try plane is used for obtaining a straight edge on long pieces of timber; as

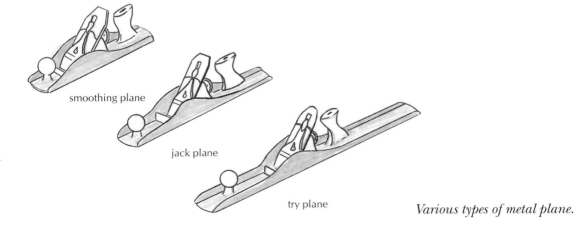

smoothing plane

jack plane

try plane

Various types of metal plane.

The parts of a metal plane.

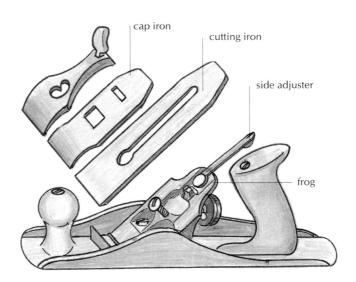

when joining planks together to make a tabletop. The jack plane is for general-purpose planing and the smoothing plane, as the name implies, is for finishing work off before scraping and sanding. These three planes vary in size but are maintained, set and used in the same way and so one description will suffice for all.

The blade of the plane is in two parts: the cutting iron and the cap iron. These are held together with a screw that passes through the cutting iron. The cap iron needs to fit snugly against the cutting iron or the blade will clog; it also needs to be adjusted closer to the end of the cutting iron when planing hardwood than when planing softwood. The assembled blade is fitted on to an assembly on the main body of the plane called the 'frog'. The frog is fitted with a wheel assembly to adjust the depth of cut and a lever that provides a side-to-side movement of the blade.

To set the blade for depth of cut, sight along the bottom or sole of the plane and turn the blade adjuster until the blade just appears below the bottom. While sighting in this way, with the blade just appearing, move the side-to-side adjuster until an even amount of blade appears on both sides. It may be necessary to readjust depth again once the blade is level.

PLANING

When planing it is important to stand in a comfortable position and to have the work firmly held, either in a vice or cramp or against a bench stop. When the plane is first brought into contact with the wood

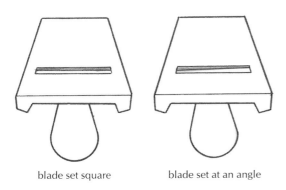

blade set square   blade set at an angle

View along the bottom of the plane to check that the blade projects equally across the mouth.

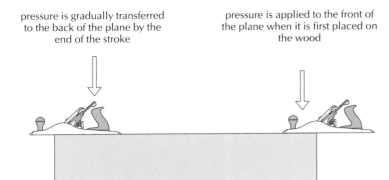

pressure is gradually transferred to the back of the plane by the end of the stroke

pressure is applied to the front of the plane when it is first placed on the wood

The pressure is transferred from the front to the back of the plane.

pressure is applied with the left hand at the front of the plane, so as to keep it flat on the work right from the start. This pressure should be gradually transferred to the other hand by the end of the stroke. When

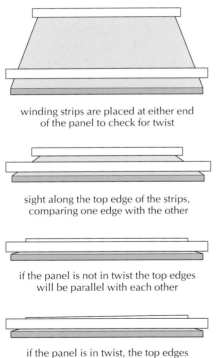

winding strips are placed at either end of the panel to check for twist

sight along the top edge of the strips, comparing one edge with the other

if the panel is not in twist the top edges will be parallel with each other

if the panel is in twist, the top edges will not be parallel

Using the winding strips.

planing the edge of a piece of wood there is always a tendency to plane the surface convex by taking more wood off at the end of the stroke. This may be overcome by using as long a plane as possible and trying to plane in a hollow or concave manner.

The straightness of the work should be constantly checked. On short pieces of work this can be done by tipping the plane so that the edge of the sole or base of the plane can be used as a straight edge; on longer pieces it will be necessary to sight along the edge. To sight for straightness simply close one eye and 'spy' along the edge of the wood; in this way the slightest irregularity will be detected.

On wider pieces of work, such as panels, it will be necessary to check for 'twist', for which winding strips are employed. These are two strips of wood, usually about 18in long, 2in wide and ½in thick ($460 \times 50 \times 12$mm); the top edges are sometimes bevelled to make them thinner. The winding strips are placed on the work, one at either end, so that it is possible to sight across the top surfaces. The strips will exaggerate the amount of twist, making it easy to detect. It is not possible to measure the amount of twist so an amount will have to be planed off and the test carried out again.

It should be noted here that it is not necessary to check very thin panels for twist since these are easily bent to the correct position when the work is assembled. Once the face is out of twist and straight it should be face-marked with a loop, the tails of which point towards the face edge.

SQUARING THE EDGE

Select the better edge and place the work in the vice if it is thin, or place it against a bench stop if it is thick enough to stand up while being planed. It is a good practice to hold the plane with the fingers of the left hand gliding along the face so that the plane can be held at right angles to the face just planed. Check for straightness as described earlier and check for squareness to the face by the use of a square. When using the square, always remember that 'stock and faces go together'. Place the stock of the square against the face side of the work and sight by holding the work with the square in place up towards the light, so that any light can be seen between the edge of the timber and the blade of the square. Either slide the square along the work or test at intervals. If it is not square, plane the prominent part; if it is correct mark with a large 'V', pointing towards the face side.

PLANING TO THE CORRECT WIDTH AND THICKNESS

Now we come to the second edge. Set a marking gauge to the desired width and mark on the face side, with the stock against the face edge. Plane this second edge to the line, checking at intervals that it is square to the face side, in the same way as was done for the first edge.

We then come to the last side, or the back of the work. Set the marking gauge to the desired thickness and mark both edges from the face side. Plane to the gauged line and test with the edge of the plane for straightness across the face to make sure that you have not left too much wood in the middle. When this has been done, the timber is said to be 'trued up', that is, that it is straight, out of twist, square and of the desired size. In making any article the pieces for the framework are first trued up; they are then 'set out' for jointing, moulding or some other process, after which the item is assembled and finished off.

The quality of the finishing off will depend on the quality of the work. Rough work may be left just planed ready for the application of wood preserver or exterior wood stain. Painted work is usually planed and sandpapered; polished hardwood is planed, scraped and sanded.

SMOOTHING OR FINISHING

After an item has been assembled it will need to be finished off and this is done with the smoothing plane. The two most important points to remember are, first, that the blade must be set to cut as finely as

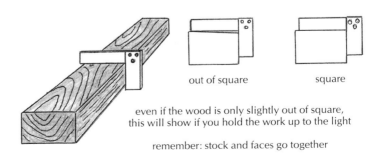

Checking for square.

out of square   square

even if the wood is only slightly out of square, this will show if you hold the work up to the light

remember: stock and faces go together

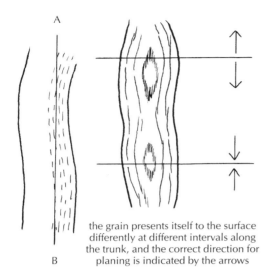

the grain presents itself to the surface differently at different intervals along the trunk, and the correct direction for planing is indicated by the arrows

Planing must be in the direction of grain.

direction for planing does not depend upon the shape of the grain lines but on how the grain rises to the surface of the wood. When you plane against the direction of the grain there is a tendency for the grain to 'pluck up'. It can be seen from the illustration to the left that if the trunk of the tree were cut through A–B the grain would present itself to the surface differently at different intervals along the trunk; the correct direction for planing is indicated by the arrows.

The illustration below shows two planks of wood that appear to have a very similar grain on the surface, but by examining the sides of the planks it can be seen that the grain presents itself differently and so the planks would have to be planed differently.

possible; that is, the iron should project as little beyond the sole of the plane as is consistent with removing a suitable shaving. Secondly, it is necessary to plane in the direction of the grain. There is some confusion about just what planing in the direction of the grain really means. The

PLANING END GRAIN

When planing the end of a plank of wood it is not possible simply to plane right across as if one were planing the side because a piece would splinter away from the far end. There are several methods of planing end grain to prevent this from

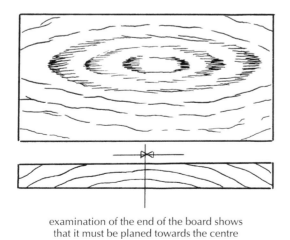

examination of the end of the board shows that it must be planed towards the centre

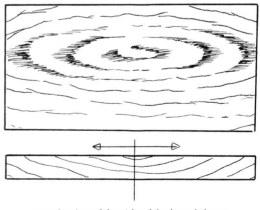

examination of the side of the board shows that it must be planed away from the centre

Similar looking grain may have to be planed in different directions.

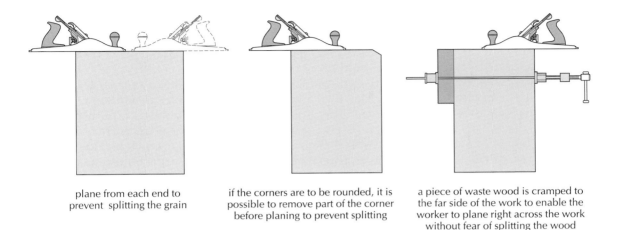

plane from each end to prevent splitting the grain

if the corners are to be rounded, it is possible to remove part of the corner before planing to prevent splitting

a piece of waste wood is cramped to the far side of the work to enable the worker to plane right across the work without fear of splitting the wood

Planing end grain.

happening. The first is simply to plane from both ends, planing just over halfway from each direction. The second is to chisel a small corner off the far end, as shown; however, this method is obviously no good if the end is to be left square. The third is to cramp a piece of waste wood on the end of the piece being planed so that it is the waste timber that splits. The fourth is to use a shooting board.

THE SHOOTING BOARD

The shooting board illustrated below is a flat piece of board with another laid on its top a few inches short of the first in width. This allows a plane to be laid on its side on the first board with the top one acting as a fence that the plane can run against. A little way in from one end a stop is let in to the upper board. This must stand up proud of the second board by at least the

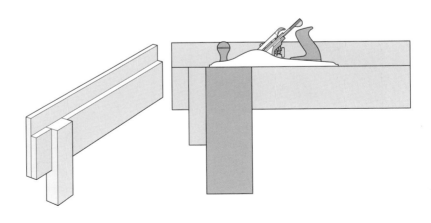

Planing end grain on the shooting board.

the shooting board

the shooting board with work in place

thickness of any wood that will be planed on the board, because if the wood being planed stands proud of the stop then the end will still split out when it is planed. To use the shooting board the work is held by hand, flat against the stop with the end to be planed flush with the side of the top board. The plane is then run along the fence as the work is pushed against it. Shooting boards may also be made with the fence let in at 45 degrees for adjusting mitres.

SPECIAL PLANES

THE TOOTHING PLANE

The toothing plane is much like a wooden smoothing plane in appearance, but with a much more upright blade. The iron itself is grooved at the back so that when it is sharpened the cutting edge is toothed. Because of the serrations at the back of the blade it is not possible to remove the burr formed during sharpening on an oilstone in the usual way. After the blade has been sharpened on the stone it is driven into the end grain of a piece of waste softwood to remove any burr.

the toothing plane has a much more upright blade than a conventional plane

the toothing iron has a serrated back, that gives it its teeth

The toothing plane.

The plane is used chiefly to roughen up a surface that is to be veneered.

THE COMPASS PLANE

The compass plane has a curved sole, usually convex for planing inside curves. The most useful is the metal, adjustable, compass plane that can be adapted to fit almost any curve, concave or convex. The blades of these planes are adjusted in exactly the same way as with conventional planes.

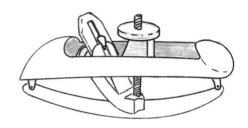

The compass plane.

THE SPOKESHAVE

A spokeshave may be described as a double-handled plane used for planing curved surfaces. It can be purchased with either a wooden or a metal body; some of the metal-bodied ones come with a screw adjustment. They are useful for cleaning up small curves which a compass plane cannot cope with, putting chamfers on

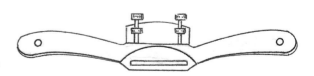

The spokeshave.

curved surfaces and shaping larger items such as cabriole legs.

MOULDING PLANES

Wooden moulding planes are no longer much used, having been largely superseded by electric routers; but a couple of differently curved planes may still be useful for a small job when it may not be worth the time to set up a machine. They are adjusted in the same way as other wooden planes. When planing mouldings it is best to start near the far end and gradually work away from it with each successive stroke.

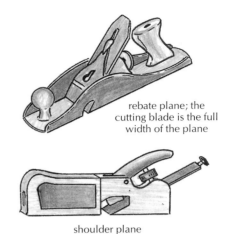

rebate plane; the cutting blade is the full width of the plane

shoulder plane

Metal rebate and shoulder planes.

THE SHOULDER PLANE

This is a narrow rebate plane that is useful for cleaning up the shoulders of tenons. The shoulder rebate plane now often comes with an interchangeable front section, giving a choice of standard or short nose for stopped rebates.

THE PLOUGH

The plough is a rebate plane with a movable fence and is used for making grooves

A moulding plane.

THE REBATE OR RABBIT PLANE

This type has a blade that extends to the edge of the plane and is used mostly for cleaning up rebates that have been cut on a circular saw. Sometimes a stop rebate is required and to be able to clean up nearer to the end of the rebate a bull-nose plane is required; this is simply a rebate plane with the blade very near its front.

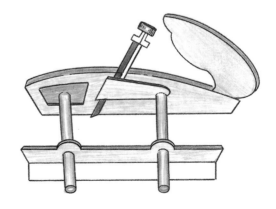

A plough plane.

and rebates. These planes have now been largely superseded by machinery.

THE BLOCK PLANE

This is a small metal plane that may be used one-handed and is useful for mitres; the width of the mouth can be adjusted by means of the screw at the front.

A block plane.

THE CABINET SCRAPER

The ordinary cabinet scraper is a piece of hard steel about 4in long, 3in wide and ⅟₁₆ in thick (100 × 76 × 2mm). It is used for the final cleaning up of hardwood after the use of the smoothing plane and before sanding. Proper use of the scraper will remove a fine shaving of timber and will save greatly on the use of sandpaper. In order to work effectively the edges of the scraper have to be sharpened and burred over. To sharpen the scraper it is necessary first to turn back any burr that has been on there previously. Lay the tool flat on the bench and hold it flat with one hand. Select a piece of hard, round steel, such as the back of a gouge, and run this flat along the full length of the scraper, repeating the operation on all four edges, lubricating with a little light oil. It is then necessary to file the

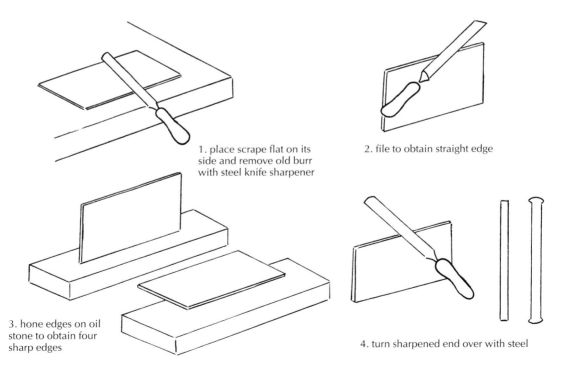

1. place scrape flat on its side and remove old burr with steel knife sharpener

2. file to obtain straight edge

3. hone edges on oil stone to obtain four sharp edges

4. turn sharpened end over with steel

Sharpening a cabinet scrape.

edges with a fine file to make sure that they are straight and then to sharpen them on the edge of an oilstone as shown. First hold the scraper on its edge, run it a few times over the stone and then remove the burr by rubbing it flat on the stone. You may find it beneficial to lubricate the steel with a little light oil for the following operations. It is now necessary to burr the edges over. This is accomplished by gripping the scraper securely in one hand and rubbing the steel firmly along the full length of the scraper, starting with the steel at right angles to the scraper, but gradually rolling it from one side to the other by about 10 to 20 degrees to burr the edges over on both sides.

When the scraper becomes blunt for the first time after the sharpening process just described it may not be necessary again to go through the whole procedure. It is possible just to flatten out the burr and then to re-burr the edge as described. This shortened sharpening procedure can usually be done a couple of times before a full sharpening becomes necessary.

When in use the scraper is held in both hands with the thumbs at the back and in the centre while the fingers are curled around the ends. Bend the scraper a little and incline it slightly forward while pushing it away from you over the surface of the wood, at which time it will remove a very fine shaving. This is so fine that the scraper can be used at a slight angle to the line of the grain; it may be an advantage to do this when removing a dent or blemish from the surface.

THE SCRATCH STOCK

The scratch stock is essentially a shaped scraper which is used for making small mouldings; indeed, in many instances the end of a cabinet scraper may be used. The scraper is filed to the required shape and secured in a piece of wood designed to act

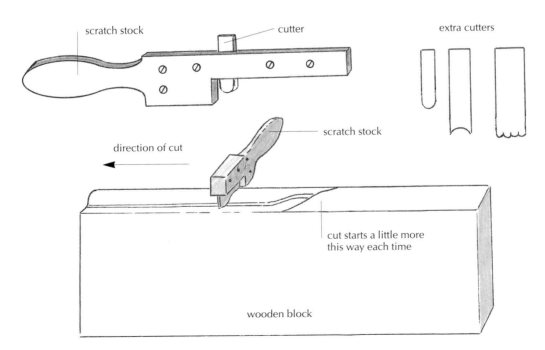

The scratch stock.

as both a handle and a guide. Very small mouldings can be produced with the use of the scratch stock alone. The shoulder of the stock is held against the side of the work and the blade presented to the work a little way in from the far end. The stock is pushed away from you towards the far end, taking off a small shaving. The stock is then pulled back, being kept firmly against the side of the work but with the cutter lifted clear, cutting taking place only on the forward stroke. Once again the cutter is presented to the work, but this time a little further away from the far end and nearer to you. The process is repeated, each time taking a little more wood and starting further away from the far end until the moulding is completed.

For larger mouldings the bulk of the waste timber will need to be removed by other means before the scratch stock is used. This may be achieved with a plane in the case of most small mouldings, but in the case of large, elaborate ones a circular saw may be employed.

MAKING MOULDINGS

Most mouldings will be cut with a router or spindle moulder; but there will be occasions when either a cutter of the correct shape is not available or when only a small amount of moulding is required when it makes more sense to cut the moulding by hand.

The wood from which the moulding is to be cut needs to be straight-grained and trued up, just as with any other component. The exact profile of the moulding is clearly marked on both ends of the wood and, in the case of larger mouldings, the bulk of the waste timber removed. With a very shallow moulding it may be sufficient to chamfer off the waste, but with deeper mouldings it is best to cut a series of grooves, either with a plough plane or on a circular saw. These grooves should be cut to the full depth of the lines to form guides

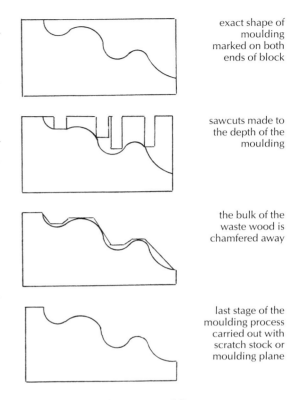

exact shape of moulding marked on both ends of block

sawcuts made to the depth of the moulding

the bulk of the waste wood is chamfered away

last stage of the moulding process carried out with scratch stock or moulding plane

Four steps to making a moulding.

as to the depths of the several hollows. The next step is to chamfer away the waste to form the section shown in the illustration. Only a little work is then needed with a scratch stock or moulding plane to finish the shaping. All procedures, such as grooving and chamfering, should be taken to the line straight off, do not be tempted to leave a little on to be cleaned up at a later stage as this creates only more work.

CURVED MOULDING

The working of curved mouldings differs from the procedures just described in that it is not possible to use the saw to cut grooves. The scratch stock is employed for the final cleaning up but the waste timber is removed with the appropriate gouge, spokeshave or carving chisel, the exact shape of the moulding having been marked clearly on both ends of the wood.

MAKING SHAPED CUTTERS

When shaping a scratch stock to cut a moulding the exact counterpart of the moulding is reproduced on the steel cutter, because the scratch stock presents itself to the work at roughly a right angle. This is not the case if the cutter is fitted into a moulding plane, which will present the cutter to the wood at an angle or pitch of about 45 degrees. A cutter that is the counterpart of the moulding will not cut a replica of it because the pitch of the blade would cause it to lose its dimensions, the depth of the moulding would be shallower and the curve flatter. This may be better understood, if you consider the case of a 25mm dowel with the end cut at an angle of 45 degrees and inserted into in a 25mm hole. Although the end of the dowel is, in fact, elliptical, every point on its circumference will touch the inside of the hole into which it fits. It may then be clearly seen that to cut a round mould, with a blade inclined at 45 degrees, the blade will need to be elliptical in shape.

To draw the shape of a cutter required for a particular moulding you first need to draw the section of the moulding to full scale and erect a vertical line X–Y, just touching the edge of the moulding. Draw the line A–B at right angles to X–Y, intersecting it at O. From O draw in the pitch of the blade or cutter. This is measured with a bevel or protractor on the blade seating in the mouth of the plane to be used. Now, from a number of points on the curve of the moulding drop down vertical lines to a point where they intersect the pitch line. With O as the centre project these lines with compasses until they cut the line A–B and erect lines up from these points. From the points originally selected and projected down from the curve of the moulding, project lines across to intersect the lines just drawn. A curve drawn passing through these points will give the required shape.

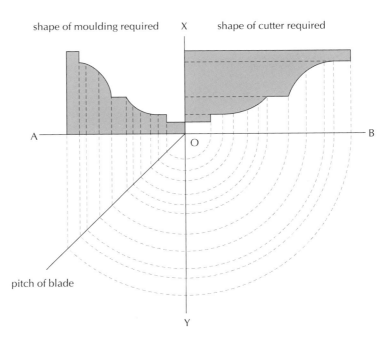

shape of moulding required   X   shape of cutter required

A ——— O ——— B

pitch of blade

Y

Determining the shape of a moulding cutter.

Timber: Its Growth and Properties

GENERAL

It is important for the woodworker to be acquainted with the natural characteristics of his chosen material; in fact, it could be argued that the highest standard of workmanship cannot be attained without it. We are not concerned here with the botanical characteristics of trees, such as the shape of their leaves, their flowers or their bark. The fungi that affect timber and the insects, such as woodworm, that burrow into it, are, as a rule, not those that affect the living tree. However, the physical characteristics of wood which determine its suitability for various purposes are dependent on its mode of growth.

Woods may generally be divided into two groups: conifers, or softwood trees, which include pines, spruces, firs, larches, cedars, junipers and yews, and broad-leafed, or hardwood trees, such as oak and walnut. Conifers mostly have very narrow needle-like leaves and have their seeds on the inner surfaces of cones. With the exception of yews, conifers have wood that is rich in resin. They are fast-growing and have a simple, uniform structure and an even grain that make them generally easy to work. Broad-leafed trees have their seeds enclosed in a fruit and their leaves are generally broad with a network of branching veins. Their wood is of a more complex structure and therefore often more difficult to work.

All the higher plants start off the same when young, built of cells, minute sacs of cellulose, filled with protoplasm and combined into tissues. In the young stems the cells become elongated in the direction of growth. Those at or near the outer surface undergo a thickening of their walls with a substance that makes them highly elastic and impermeable; they lose their protoplasm and become cork. Those at the centre merely lose their protoplasm, thus becoming physiologically dead and are known as pith.

Between the young cork and the pith a ring of cellular tissue undergoes marked changes. The cells or elements from which they are formed become much elongated and in cross-section appear more or less as wedge-shaped 'bundles', with their broader ends towards the outside of the stem. The walls of some of the outer and the innermost elements in each bundle become thickened with ligno-cellulose and gradually lose their protoplasm. This change extends inwards and outwards to all the elements of the bundle, except for those forming a narrow line parallel with the circumference of the stem. This layer retains its protoplasm and persists throughout the life of the stem as a growing layer (cambium), its cells undergoing repeated division parallel to the surface of the stem. The elements of the tissue between the bundles elongate radially, that is, from the pith out, and make up what are know as the medullary or pith rays, familiar to the woodworker as 'silver grain' or 'figure'.

In the second season's growth the active division of the cambium cells extends

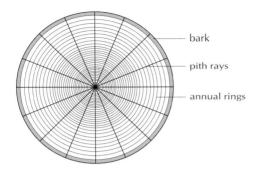

Annual rings and pith rays.

laterally in both directions across the pith rays between the bundles, so that for the first time the central portion of the stem becomes completely enveloped by a sheath of this soft, protoplasmic tissue. The portion of the stem from the cambium inwards to the pith is known as the wood.

During this second season and in each succeeding one the cambium adds new wood to the outside of the wood cylinder, at the same time adding to the pith rays and to a lesser amount to the inner bark. In temperate climates, most broad-leaved trees shed their leaves in autumn and, like conifers, go through a period of rest when neither roots nor leaves take in much food. The wood formed during these periods of rest is much reduced, and so the trunk is divided by these pauses into annual or growth rings.

SOFTWOOD

So far we have looked at how trees develop in general, and this is true for both conifer and for broad-leaved trees. When, however, we look more closely at the elements that make up the wood we have to distinguish between the relatively simple wood of the conifer and the more complex and varied wood of the broad-leafed tree. The woods of the conifers are mainly composed

of tracheides, interrupted only by resin ducts and by pith rays so narrow that they are not recognizable to the naked eye.

HARDWOOD

In conifers, the conducting of water and the affording of structural strength are both performed by the same elements, the tracheides; however, in hardwoods these functions are separated. Vessels are always present to conduct water from the roots, but structural strength is given by wood fibres. Some cellular tissue is generally present, while tracheides may or may not be.

CONVERTING THE LOG

After a tree has been cut down it needs to be cut up into pieces of timber of a usable size; this process is known as converting the log. There are two basic methods of conversion, flat or through-and-through

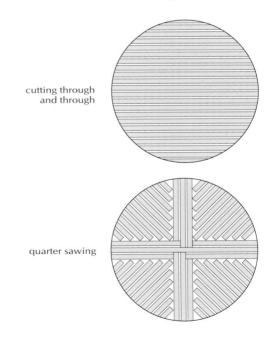

Methods of converting a log.

sawing, and quarter sawing. Through-and-through sawing is just what the name implies: the log is simply cut in slices down its length on an enormous bandsaw. This is the cheapest and easiest method of conversion, and it produces a grain that shows what is known as 'cathedral figure' because of its series of loops and arches. The grain of boards cut in this way may be easily matched if they are kept together in the order in which they were cut. Quarter-sawn wood is more expensive because it produces a large amount of waste timber, unlike the through-and-through method which produces very little. The log is first cut in half down the centre and then quartered. Each quarter section is then converted by cutting as near to parallel with the pith or medullary rays as is possible. The advantage of quarter sawing is that it dries to a much more stable condition than through-and-through sawing, making it much more suitable for structural work. Prominent pith rays show up on quarter-sawn boards as ornate silver or dark flecks in the grain.

SEASONING

The majority of woodworkers will buy their timber ready seasoned, but some who have enough storage space may like to season their own, even felling their own trees, so some explanation of the seasoning process may be helpful.

Seasoning is simply the drying-out of newly felled logs to get rid of their excessive water content. Dry wood is stronger and lighter than wet wood; it is more easily worked; takes glue, preservatives and finishes much better; and is much less likely to expand or contract. Very small logs, that is to say, logs of less than 6in (150mm) diameter, may be dried before conversion, but anything larger will need to be converted first. The most natural method of seasoning

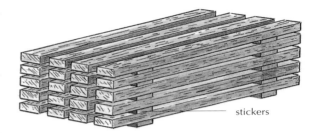

the stack should be at least 500mm (20in) off the ground and under cover to prevent it getting wet

Timber sawn and stacked for seasoning.

is air drying, allowing the sun and wind to do the work. For air drying, as with any other method, the wood must be stacked in such a way as to allow for the free passage of air around the whole length of timber on both sides, and this is achieved by separating the piled up boards with 'stickers'. These are pieces of the same timber as that being seasoned, about 1×1in $(25 \times 25$mm$)$ by the width of the board. They are placed at intervals along the length of the boards to separate them and to allow air flow; however, great care must be taken to make sure that the stickers are positioned above one another and not offset, as this would cause the wood to bow. The stickers need to be the same species of timber as the wood being seasoned in order to prevent 'stick stain' that can penetrate deep into the wood and cannot be planed off. The stain is caused by a chemical reaction between the two timbers and is especially disastrous on light-coloured timber. The bottom of the timber stack should be at least 20in (50cm) off the ground and under cover to prevent its getting wet. The preferable solution is to store the timber in an open-sided barn, but a tarpaulin rigged in such a way that it does not interfere with the flow of air will suffice. Timber will have a tendency to dry quicker towards the ends than in the middle, and painting the ends of the boards will help to even the drying out.

MOISTURE CONTENT

How much timber is seasoned, or how dry we make it depends upon the purpose for which it will be used. The dryness is defined as moisture content or MC. Air drying can achieve a moisture content of 18 per cent, which is suitable for exterior joinery; but for timber to be used in the manufacture of furniture or in a building that will be regularly heated the moisture content has to be reduced further, to more like 12 per cent, by kiln drying.

KILN DRYING

Proper kiln drying requires much knowledge and expertise, especially if more than one type of wood is being seasoned at a time. Once timber has been air dried to 18 per cent MC the moisture content can be reduced further by stacking it in a confined space with a dehumidifier for several weeks. It will, of course, be necessary to purchase an electrical moisture meter for testing the moisture content at intervals.

SHRINKAGE

Wood shrinks when it loses water, but not the free water in the cavities of the wood elements but that which saturates the cell walls. This shrinkage will mainly effect the width of the timber, but the length only a little.

SPLITTING OR CHECKING

The more rapidly wood is dried the greater tendency there is for it to split. Splits usually occur in the direction of the pith ray and along the grain. Normally end splits may be ignored; cut off and discarded as waste, unless they are severe.

WARPING

If a board is cut by the through-and-through method and has been inadequately seasoned, cupping will occur. The side of the board which was nearer to the outside of the tree in life will shrink more than the side which was nearer to the pith, and become concave.

BOW

Bow occurs when the edges of the board remain flat but the face becomes arched.

CUPPING

This occurs when one side of a board shrinks more than the other. Shrinkage will be greater on the side of the board that was nearer to the outside of the tree.

SPRING

Spring occurs when the face of the board remains flat and the sides become arched.

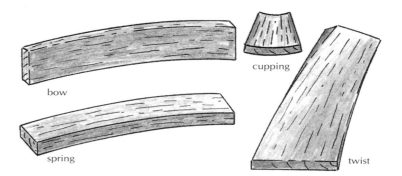

Defects in seasoned timber.

TWIST

Twist is present when neither the sides nor the faces remain flat.

MANUFACTURED BOARD

These days the woodworker does not need to confine his choice of material to natural timber since there are a variety of manufactured boards on the market. These are available in large, well prepared sheets that are more stable than natural timber. The main ones are described here.

BLOCKBOARD

Blockboard is made up of strips of wood which are laid parallel to each other. They then have veneers laid on each side with the grain running at 90 degrees to each of them. This is a relatively cheap board that is light in weight and takes both nails and screws well. Blockboard is used mainly for structural panelling; housing joints and dowels are suitable when joining blockboard.

PLYWOOD

Plywood is made up of sheets of veneer with the grain successively alternating by 90 degrees from one sheet to the next. It is the strongest of the manufactured boards and in thinner boards the most bendable, making it suitable for covering a variety of curved surfaces. It takes nails and screws well, except at its ends, and can be jointed in a variety of ways, including dovetailing. Thicker plywoods may be expensive but are very stable; thinner plywood is ideal for curved work.

There are usually odd numbers of layers – three-ply, five-ply, multi-ply, for instance – in each plywood, of which there are the following types.

Marine Plywood
The most durable type, with a very strong bond between the layers, which should be able to withstand exterior exposure.

Structural Plywood
This should be able to withstand a certain amount of pressure and load and is suitable for wall panelling, hoardings, flooring and roof decking.

Non-Structural Plywood
This is used in joinery, shop-fitting and cabinet-making, and is available with a variety of decorative face veneers.

PARTICLE BOARD

Particle board, or chipboard as it is more commonly known, comes in various forms. Single-layer chipboard is composed of wood chips of similar size, lying parallel to the plane of the board. Three-ply chipboard consists of an inner core of large particles, with an outer layer of finer particles on either side, giving a smoother surface. Graded-density chipboard has a centre of large particles, an outer surface of very fine particles, the particles in between having a gradation in size. Chipboard is the cheapest of the boards but also the weakest and the least resistant to bending, making it unsuitable for shelving or weight-bearing of any kind. It is often used for flooring and is veneered for cabinet making; however, it is unsuitable for nailing and should be reinforced with a dowel or plastic bush before screwing. Chipboard is suitable only for use in dry situations.

FIBRE BOARD

Several types of fibre board are available. Insulation board is a low-density board used for sound and heat insulation that can be purchased in sheet or tile form. Hardboard is a thin, dense board, with one smooth side.

It is used as a floor covering and in furniture manufacture for cabinet backs and drawer bottoms. Medium-density fibre board, or MDF, is the latest manufactured board and is now extensively used in furniture manufacture. MDF is a very useful board which takes screws well if pilot-drilled first; it may be moulded, jointed and takes finishes well. The drawback to MDF is the fact that it quickly takes the edge off tools, and there are some health fears associated with it, so that it is strongly recommended that a mask should be worn when cutting the material. There is an MDF board that is moisture-resistant (MDFMR) which can be used for staircases, window boards, skirting boards, fascias and soffits.

JOINING BLOCKS

There are several plastic corner blocks on the market which have been designed for joining manufactured boards to make carcase construction easy.

WOOD ROT AND INSECT ATTACK

ROT

All external timber needs protection from the weather in one way or another. Rain will cause wood to expand, the sun will dry it out and make it contract as well as bleaching out its natural colour. The real enemies, however, are rot and insect attack and it is necessary to take precautions against these from day one. One of the most fundamental precautions which can be taken is in the actual design of exterior items. Avoid any perfectly flat horizontal surface where water may accumulate. The tops of posts should be covered with a cap to protect the end grain, and all gate and fence rails should be bevelled so that water runs straight off them. Any split or gap between timbers where moisture could penetrate should be filled. However, even well-designed exterior woodwork will still need protection with some kind of wood finish, be it oil, paint or an exterior varnish stain.

KNOW YOUR ENEMY

FUNGI

The life cycle of a fungus is simple. A mature fruiting body or sporophore will give off spores, and these will be transported by wind, an insect or an animal to another suitable piece of damp timber where germination can take place. The fungus will then spread its roots into and along the timber in search of food. It will continue to grow if the conditions are right until it in turn produces a fruiting body. The main types of fungus that concern the woodworker are described below.

Blue Stain
Blue stain, as its name implies, causes the blue stain which is sometimes seen on softwoods. Although unsightly, this fungus does not significantly damage timber and so it may still be apparent in timber yards.

Wet Rot
Wet rot is the most common type of rot that we see around the home. As the name indicates, this type of rot needs a high moisture content to survive and is most often found in places where water is allowed to accumulate, such as window sills, beneath leaking pipes and in areas of high condensation. If left unchecked, wet rot will completely destroy timber, but fortunately it is relatively easy to eradicate.

To get rid of wet rot it is necessary first to find and remove the cause of the damp. Once this has been done any really badly

47

affected timber will have to be cut out and replaced. A bradawl or other pointed tool is used to check the timber to see how badly it is affected. In rotten wood the bradawl will sink into the timber with hardly any effort, but more will be needed in timber that is less or only partially infected. It is best if all the bad area is replaced back to sound timber. The replacement timber will need to be of a low moisture content and treated with an appropriate wood pre-server, as will any of the original sound tim-ber left behind. Areas that were only slightly affected can, once they are thor-oughly dried out, be treated with a wood preserver and hardener, have any splits filled with wood stopper and be painted over. Probably the biggest danger associ-ated with wet rot is the possibility that in certain circumstances it may be taken over by dry rot, a much more serious condition.

Dry Rot

Dry rot develops where there is a high moisture content coupled with poor venti-lation. It is a far bigger and more insidious problem than wet rot and much harder to eradicate. The fungus has moisture-con-ducting strands that enable it to travel behind plaster and even through walls in its relentless search for food and sources of moisture. Dry rot is a master at hiding away, and often the first indication that there is a problem is its characteristic, mushroom-like odour or a slightly dis-torted skirting board, or panel. To pull up floorboards and discover dry rot is a horri-ble experience indeed, since you may well be confronted with a huge expanse of the soft, white fungus and possibly also a red, fleshy, fruiting body which is capable of producing millions of spores.

The eradication of dry rot is a major undertaking, even with quite small out-breaks the size of the task should not be underestimated. As with the eradication of wet rot, the source of the initial dampness

must be found and rectified. All timber to within 50cm (20in) but preferably 1m (40in) must be removed and incinerated. Great care must be taken in the trans-portation of infected timber not to spread the spores to unaffected areas. Check with the local authority, since they may need to approve the method and location of the disposal of infected timber. Any plaster must be removed from walls within 50cm of the last sign of infection and all brick-work and walls must be treated with an appropriate fungicide. Replacement tim-ber must have a low moisture content and be treated with a wood preserver and fungicide, especially on its end grain. One of the best ways of ensuring that reinfesta-tion does not occur is to make sure that the area is well ventilated. Adequate ventila-tion will keep down the moisture content.

INSECTS

COMMON FURNITURE BEETLE

This is the most common of the wood-bor-ing insects. The adult beetle is reddish- to blackish-brown in colour and 3 to 5mm (about 0.2in) in length. The adult beetle lives for about thirty days but the life cycle is around two years. The adult female bee-tle will lay her eggs in a small hole or gap in furniture after mating. The resulting lar-vae bore their way into the wood and may remain there, causing considerable dam-age, for up to two years, at which time they make their way to just beneath the surface of the wood. Here they create a small chamber in which to pupate (change into chrysalides). When the transformation from larvae to beetle is complete, usually between May and August, they bite their way out, leaving a flight hole some 1 to 2mm (about 0.1in) in diameter, and the cycle is repeated.

— 8 —

Drawing for Woodworkers

Some knowledge of drawing and elementary plane geometry are necessary for the woodworker to enable him to prepare and read drawings and to set work out. Every workshop should have the basic drawing instruments: a drawing board, a T-square, set squares, a scale rule, compasses and dividers.

Most of the drawings that you will encounter in woodwork will be drawn to scale. If you receive the plans of a window or a cabinet which has to be made it is inconceivable that these plans would be full size and so some knowledge of scale drawing is required.

Below are the dimensions of a fitted corner wardrobe and we shall go through the drawing of the plans of it step by step. The wardrobe is 2,220mm (87.4in) tall by 1,600mm (63.0in) wide by 1,100mm (43.7in) deep and is fitted with three doors which are each 497mm (19.6in) wide and 2,020mm (79.5in) high.

The tools required to make the plan are a drawing board and T-square, some paper on which to draw the plan, a sharp, hard pencil, a set square and a scale rule. Compasses and dividers are also essential drawing equipment. The traditional wooden drawing board and T-square are now often given up in favour of modern drawing boards with a built-in square for horizontal lines. Scale rules can be purchased in either the flat, traditional rule shape or in a triangular form.

The scales will be marked from 1:2.5, meaning that 1cm on the drawing represents 2.5cm in full size; 1:5 meaning that 1cm on the drawing represents 5cm in full size; 1:10 meaning that 1cm on the drawing represents 10cm in full size, and so on up to 1:100 meaning that 1cm on the drawing represents 100cm or 1m in full size. The particular scale used for any drawing should be marked on the drawing, together with any other information, such as the title and number, the date the drawing was made and the location of the project.

Drawing paper comes in sizes ranging from A6, the smallest at 148mm × 105mm, through A5, A4, A3, A2 and A1 up to the massive A0 at 1,189mm × 841mm. For our wardrobe plan A3 paper (420mm × 297mm) will be used.

First we have to provide some space on the paper for a title panel and an information panel. These are usually situated down the right-hand side of the paper. Draw a line down this side of the paper about one-quarter of the way in, and then divide this panel into two with a horizontal line about one-third of the way up from the bottom of the page. The smaller bottom panel is the title panel and in here you should write the drawing title, the number if it has one, the date and, most important, the scale used. We shall be using a scale of 1:20. The top information panel is for any information which will be of use to whoever is to make the wardrobe from the drawing. Two pieces of information that will be required are the material from which the wardrobe is to be constructed and how it is to be finished.

Now that has been done we must visualize how the drawing is to be laid out on the paper. It is no good starting to draw the front elevation in the middle of the paper if that will not leave enough room for the side elevation without encroaching on the title panel.

There are several different drawing projections that can be used, but the most common are: first angle orthographic projection, third angle orthographic projection and isometric projection.

ISOMETRIC PROJECTION

In isometric projection the wardrobe is viewed from a corner with all perpendicular lines drawn as such and the base sides projected out at 30 degrees in each direction. All lines that are parallel to the base line are also then drawn at 30 degrees. This differs from perspective drawing where all lines that are parallel would be directed to a vanishing point on the horizon. The first line to be drawn is the inner corner. The line is drawn perpendicular, at first only faintly, and its length is marked with dividers which have be opened to the correct distance against the scale rule. It is more accurate to mark with the dividers in this way than to place the rule on the paper; however, this may be done if it is preferred. The top and the bottom line of the long front of the wardrobe are then drawn away to the left at 30 degrees. The short front can then be projected away to the right, also at 30 degrees, and the drawing continued as shown.

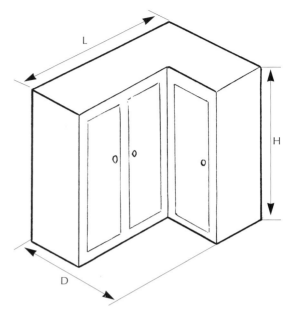

A corner wardrobe.

Dimensions are placed on the drawing by extending the lines beyond the cabinet, but leaving a gap so that it is obvious that the line does not form part of the structure. Dimension lines are then drawn between them with an arrowhead at each end and the dimension drawn in the middle. It is important when reading a drawing to distinguish between individual and

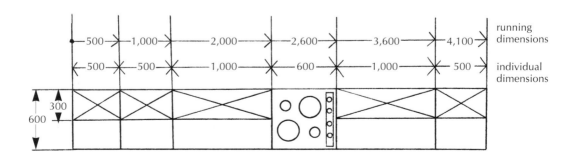

Running and individual dimensions.

running dimensions. Individual dimensions are simply the dimensions between the two dimension lines, whereas running dimensions are the sums of all the dimensions from a single datum point.

FIRST ANGLE PROJECTION

End elevation D is drawn to the right of the front elevation, and end elevation C to its left (see overleaf). The plan is drawn directly below the front elevation. When the position of the front elevation has been decided, begin by drawing a faint line, with the T-square. Continue this line on either side, past the points where the side elevations will be. Open the dividers to 1,600mm (63in) on the scale rule, remembering to use the 1:20 scale, and mark this on the faint line just drawn as the overall width of the front elevation. Go over the faint line with the hard pencil again between these two marks. Now, resting the set square on the T-square, draw a faint, perpendicular line up from each end of the wardrobe base. Open the dividers to 2,220mm (87.4in) on the scale rule and mark the height of the wardrobe on each line. Now join the two marks you have just made with a faint line and continue it out on either side, past the point of the side elevations. Go over the lines again between these marks and the outline of the front elevation is complete.

The depth of the wardrobe sides is 600mm (23.6in), so open the dividers to this scale dimension and, with one point on the right-hand side, mark this distance in, on the top and the bottom line. With the set square, join these to marks to show the position of the corner. Mark the positions of the two doors that show on the front elevation and draw them in; once again these lines may be continued faintly past the position

for the side elevations. The perpendicular lines of the front elevation may be extended down, faintly, past the point where the plan is to be drawn, and the plan then drawn. Note that the doors are shown partially open, with a curved arc. This is the standard way to show a door and the direction of its opening on a plan.

Now if lines are drawn at 45 degrees from each of the two bottom, outermost corners of the front elevation, lines from the plan may be extended to these 45-degree lines and then projected up to form the perpendicular lines of the side elevations. These lines together with the one projected across from the front elevation will produce the side elevations. Hidden details, such as the corner line on side elevation C, are shown as a dotted line. Interior shelves could also be drawn as dotted lines, as could the door. It is important to include as much information on the drawing as is possible, without making it too complicated to understand.

THIRD ANGLE PROJECTION

Third angle projection is drawn in exactly the same way as first angle projection, except for the fact that the end elevations are shown on the opposite sides.

POSSIBLE PROBLEMS

This section provides notes on some of the basic problems that you may meet in setting out work.

To bisect a line (see overleaf, top left): the line AB is required to be divided into two equal parts. Place the point of the compass on A, and open to a distance rather more than half the length AB. Scribe the arc CD

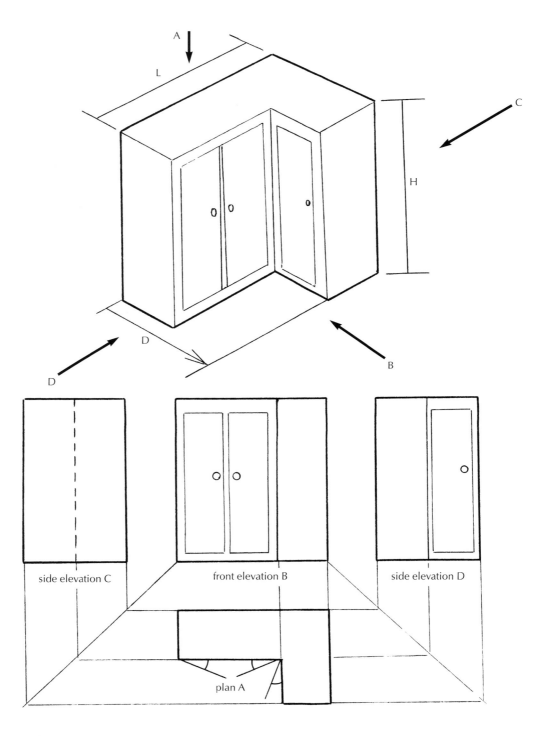

First angle projection.

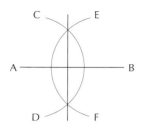

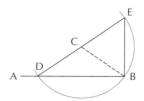

To erect a perpendicular line from the end of another.

To bisect a line.

and then, with the point of the compass on *B*, scribe the arc *EF*. A line drawn connecting the points where the two arcs meet will equally divide *AB*.

To erect a perpendicular line from the end of another (*see* above right): draw the line *AB*. Place the point of the compass *C* at any point above the line and extend the pencil point of the compass until it reaches *B* and scribe part of a circle until it cuts the line *AB* at *D*. Draw a line from *D*, through *C* until it meets the arc at *E*. A line then drawn from *B* to *E* will be at right angles to *AB*.

Another method of erecting a perpendicular line (*see* below): draw the line *AB*. Using dividers, divide *AB* into three equal parts by stepping out. Open the dividers to what you estimate to be one-third of its length and, placing the point on one end of the line, step out the distance. It will be found that the distance is not correct and that the

spread of the divider points will have to be increased or decreased to compensate and the line stepped out again until the spread is correct. The line *AB* is then three units long. Place the compass point on *A*, open the instrument to five units and scribe an arc at *C*. With the compass point on *B*, open the compasses to four units and scribe an arc at *C*. A line from *B* to the junction of the two arcs will be at right angles to *AB*.

Measurement of angles: an angle is formed when two straight lines meet, as shown below. The illustration shows a protractor being used to measure the angle at *C*. The protractor is placed on the line *AB* with its centre at the point where the two lines meet, *C*, and the angle may then be read off, in this case 45 degrees.

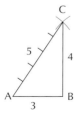

Another method of erecting a perpendicular line.

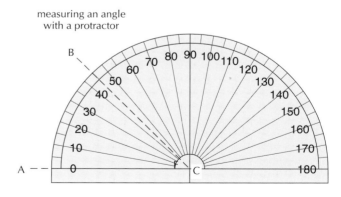

The protractor.

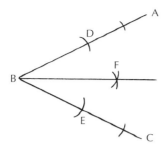

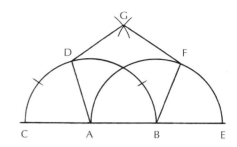

To bisect an angle.

To construct a pentagon.

To bisect an angle (*see* above): to bisect the angle *ABC*, the compass point is placed on *B* and an arc is drawn with any radius that cuts the lines *AB* and *BC* at *D* and *E*. From *D* and *E* scribe arcs of any radius that cut across each other at *F*. A line drawn from *B* to *F* will bisect the angle.

To construct a regular pentagon (*see* above right): a regular pentagon has five sides of equal length. Draw the base *AB* equal in length to one side. From *A*, with the radius *AB*, scribe a semicircle and extend the line *AB* to meet the semicircle at *C*. Divide the semicircle into five equal parts by stepping off with dividers, and from *A* draw *AD* to the second division. With the radius *AB*, scribe the semicircle *AE* and extend the line *AB* to *E*. With the compass point on *E*

and the diameter *CD*, scribe an arc cutting the semicircle at *F* and draw the line *BF*. From *D* and *F* with the diameter *AD* scribe arcs crossing at *G* and draw the lines *GD* and *GF* to complete the figure.

To construct a regular hexagon (*see* below left): a regular hexagon has six sides of equal length. Draw the line *AB* equal in length to one side. Scribe arcs from *A* and *B* with the diameter *AB* and crossing at *O*. From *O* scribe a circle with the same diameter. Divide this into six equal parts by scribing arcs from *A* to *C*, *B* to *D*, *D* to *F* and from *C* to *E*. Join these points to form the hexagon.

To draw an ellipse (*see* below): draw the major diameter of the ellipse *AB*. Bisect *AB* at *E* and draw the minor diameter *CD*. With

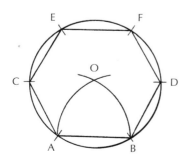

To form a hexagon.

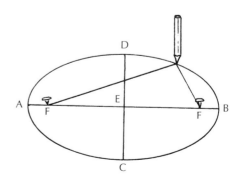

To draw an ellipse.

the radius *EA* and from the point *D* scribe a semicircle cutting the long diameter at the foci *FF*. (These are the two points on the major diameter of an ellipse to which, if radii are drawn to them from any given point on the circumference, the sum of their lengths will be equal to the length of the major diameter.) Place a pin at each point *F* and another at *D*. Tie one end of a piece of string to one pin at *F*, pass it over *D* and tie it off at the second pin *F*, forming a triangle. Take out the pin at *D* and place a pencil there in its stead. The pencil can then be drawn along the inside of the string loop and will trace an ellipse.

THE ROD

When the carpenter receives the drawing for a particular project the work is set out on what is known as a 'rod'. The rod is simply a board, a piece of plywood or paper on which the horizontal and the vertical sections of the work are drawn out full-size. There are no broken lines or scale measurements of any kind on the rod, so its size will depend on the size of the job in hand. If the project is a fairly large one or if the rod is to be kept and used again at a later date, it may be drawn on decorator's lining paper pinned to a board. After use, the paper may be rolled up and stored somewhere safe. The board on which the rod is drawn will have to have a planed straight edge from which a line can be squared across. Any moulding used on the work can

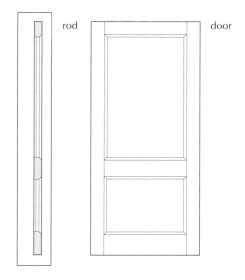

when the timber has been prepared it can be placed on the rod and 'marked off'

The rod.

also be drawn full-size on the rod so that any cutter can be made.

Once the drawing is complete the rod can be used to produce a cutting list of materials. The list should include not just the sizes of the several pieces of wood but also a description of the item it will make and the type of timber it is to be cut from. When the timber has been cut and prepared the pieces can be placed on the rod and 'marked off' showing the positions of all the joints.

— 9 —

Fixing

GLUE AND GLUING

There was a time, not all that long ago, when you used paint for sticking exterior work, animal glue for interior work and, if you wanted something different, you had to choose between a nail or a screw. These days there are so many different types of glue on the market that it is very confusing, and many of them are highly specialized, making it extremely important to pick the right one for the job. One thing that has not changed is that a joint still has to be a good fit for the glue to work well. No matter how strong it is, a thin layer of glue is all that is required. I can always remember Carlo, my tutor when I was an apprentice, telling me that there were two kinds of person in the world: those who use glue for holding wood together and those who use glue for holding wood apart! Make sure that you are one of the former and not the latter.

ANIMAL OR SCOTCH GLUE

Little used now other than for veneering and antique restoration, it gives a strong bond and has good gap-filling qualities but poor water and heat resistance. The glue is purchased in cake or pearl form and is dissolved in water. A special glue pot is required which has an inner container for the glue itself, which is suspended in an outer container that holds hot water. To mix it the glue is placed in its container, just covered with a little cold water and allowed to stand for a short while. The water in the outer container is then

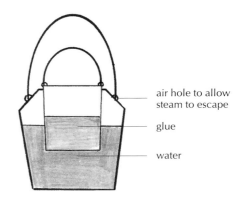

air hole to allow steam to escape

glue

water

Glue pot.

brought to the boil and more water is added to the glue. The water in the outer pot is kept as hot as possible without allowing it to boil over.

When the glue is soft it must be stirred regularly and tested for thickness by picking some up on the glue brush, and allowing it to run back into the pot. It should run off the brush in a continuous stream with no lumps and without breaking into droplets. More water or glue can be added to obtain the required consistency. When the glue is ready it is important to work quickly so that the glue does not cool before the joint is made. The working time available may be increased by a prior heating of the components to be joined; hot water should always be on hand for cleaning off any excess of glue. For the best results the joint should be kept in cramps and in a warm environment until the following day. Because Scotch glue is reversible, that is to say that the joint may be taken apart by applying heat, it is the best one to use in the restoration of antiques.

PVA GLUE (POLYVINYL ACETATE)

The most convenient and widely used woodworking glue, it comes ready for use in variously-sized containers and is suitable for all general-purpose interior work. Under normal circumstances the glue is dry within an hour or so, but it does tend to 'creep' a little under load so that it is a good idea to leave it several hours if you are going to work on the piece just jointed.

HOT-MELT GLUE

This is used in a special heat gun; it is a good, strong, water-resistant glue but has poor resistance to heat. The glue is dry and strong in about one minute, but it has only limited use in general woodwork.

UREA FORMALDEHYDE

An extremely strong, water- and heat-resistant glue that comes in a powder form and has to be mixed with water before use: the powder is added slowly to cold water while being stirred, until a creamy consistency is achieved. It is useful for exterior woodwork and joints which have to be very strong; its only drawbacks are the facts that you usually mix too much of it (which is wasteful), it has a limited shelf life and may stain the wood if it is not properly cleaned off. Joints need to be cramped while they dry and this normally takes several hours depending on the temperature.

EPOXY RESINS

Epoxy is supplied in two tubes, one of adhesive and one of hardener; these two substances are mixed together in equal quantities to prepare the adhesive. These glues give a very strong bond are useful for joining non-wooden materials such as brass, glass or plastics.

IMPACT ADHESIVES

These are mostly used in woodwork for gluing down plastic laminates and veneers to wood. They are very useful for gluing marquetry panels, when other, wet glues could cause problems of expansion in the veneer. The adhesives are supplied ready for use but give off a highly inflammable vapour and must be used in a well-ventilated area, away from any flame. To use, the glue is applied with a toothed spreader to both the surfaces to be joined; the glue is then allowed to become touch dry before the surfaces are brought together when they will bond instantly.

NAILING, SCREWING AND BOLTING

Nails are, generally speaking, used only for inferior work or for constructional carpentry; if they are used at all on quality work the nails are kept out of sight. There are different nails for different jobs, not just several sizes. The types are described below.

Round and oval wire nails: the oval nail does not hold in the wood as well as the round nail because the head of the latter assists in the holding, but it does not split the wood so easily and only leaves a small hole. The head of the round nail has a serrated top to stop the hammer from slipping off and both round and oval nails are roughened near the head to help them to hold in the wood.

Annular ringed nail: mostly used for fixing into plywood where the rings grip the fibres better than other nails; this nail is corrosion-resistant.

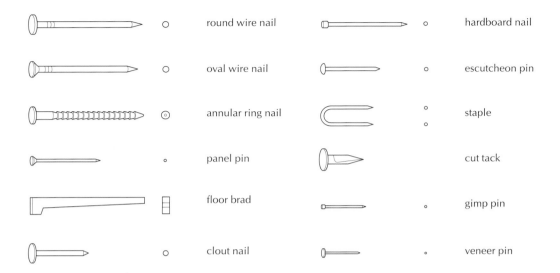

	round wire nail		hardboard nail
	oval wire nail		escutcheon pin
	annular ring nail		staple
	panel pin		cut tack
	floor brad		gimp pin
	clout nail		veneer pin

Various types of nail.

Panel pin: this is really a small, round, wire nail with a small head and is ideal for nailing moulding and small beads.

Floor brad: this type of nail is pressed out of sheet steel and is about 55mm (2.2in) in length. It is used, as the name implies, for fixing floor boards and the head is designed to embed itself in the board with the last hammer blow, eliminating the need for a nail punch.

Clout nail: this is a small, round nail with a large, flat head that makes it suitable for nailing roof felt, plasterboard and similar materials.

Hardboard nail: like a panel pin, but with a pointed head that countersinks itself without the need for a nail punch.

Escutcheon pin: used for fastening metal fittings such as handle plates and escutcheon plates to furniture.

Staple: used with a staple gun, this provides a quick method of fixing upholstery and other thin materials to wood.

Cut tacks: used in upholstery for fixing webbing and covering materials.

Gimp pin: used for attaching gimp and braid in upholstery.

HOLDING POWER

When a nail is driven into a piece of wood some of the wood fibres are broken and bent down; it is the ends of these fibres, pressing against the sides of the nail, which hold it in place. If two pieces of wood are nailed together the top piece is held by the friction on the nail's sides and the holding power of the nail head whereas the lower piece will be held only by friction. Nails should be used so that the holding power is the same for each piece of wood joined;

the holding power is that of the weakest side, just as the strength of a chain is equal only to that of the weakest link.

It follows that if a piece of wood 12mm (½in) thick is nailed to a thicker piece, the length of the nail in the lower piece should be more than 12mm in order to make up for the holding power of the nail head in the upper piece. If the nail used were an oval one with a small head, a suitable nail would be 30mm long; but if the nail were a round one with a large head a 36mm nail would be better. If two piece of equal thickness are to be joined and nails equal in length to the two thicknesses used, the nails would pull out of the back piece easily. For this reason longer nails are sometimes used and 'clinched', that is, they are driven right through and bent over on the other side.

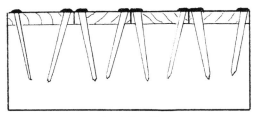

dovetail nailing

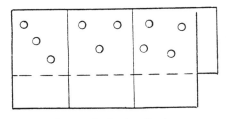

various methods of nailing to prevent splitting

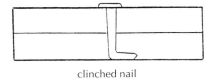

clinched nail

Methods of using nails.

Another method of increasing holding power is to drive the nails in at an angle, sometimes known as dovetail nailing. It can be seen that it would be more difficult to separate boards that have been dovetail-nailed than those which have had the nails driven in straight.

PREVENTING SPLITTING

Most softwood can be nailed without too much danger of splitting occurring, unless you are near the end of the board or several nails are put in a line. Hardwoods are always prone to splitting, and it is advisable to drill a pilot hole first, a little smaller than the diameter of the nail. In nailing boards and battens it is always better to zigzag the nails to avoid splitting, and to increase holding power. Several methods of zigzagging are shown.

HAMMERING

The actual process of hammering is quite simple and just requires some practice. The common faults are holding the hammer too near to its the head and too stiffly. The hammer should be held as near the end of the shaft as feels comfortable and be allowed to fall freely, striking the nail with a sharp rap. There must always be something substantial beneath or behind the work to absorb the impact and to prevent vibration. If it is not possible to lay the work on a sound surface, as in the case of vertical timbers, then a heavy weight or another hammer should be held behind the work. It is not the pressure of the weight but its resistance that helps; without it, twice as many blows with the hammer would be necessary and the parts would not be held together so tightly.

When driving the nail fully home there is always the danger of marking the surface of the wood, but this may be prevented by driving the nail almost home with the hammer alone and then the final blows using a nail punch. Always keep the face of the hammer head clean because a dirty head will either slip off the nail and mark the wood or cause the nail to bend.

Sometimes a nail will have to be withdrawn owing to its bending or catching a knot. The nail may be withdrawn either with the claw of a claw hammer or with the aid of a pair of pincers. When using either tool a piece of steel, such as the blade of a square, should be placed under it to prevent it from marking the work.

SECRET NAILING

Tongued and grooved timber can be secret-nailed as shown below; other timber can also be secret-nailed by having a small shaving lifted with a chisel, the nail is then driven in and the shaving glued back in place over it. A special tool for lifting these shavings is available but a chisel will usually suffice.

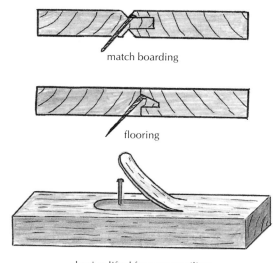

match boarding

flooring

shaving lifted for secret nailing

Secret nailing.

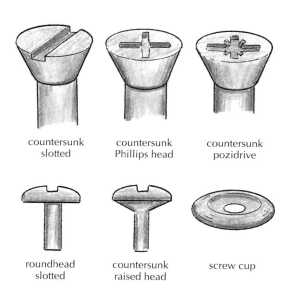

countersunk slotted   countersunk Phillips head   countersunk pozidrive

roundhead slotted   countersunk raised head   screw cup

Screw heads.

SCREWS

The advantage in use of screws over nails is twofold; first, the nail relies purely on friction whereas the screw actually pulls the two pieces together in something like a clamping action, and second, the screw is easily removed without damage to the surrounding wood. Screws come in a great variety of shapes, sizes and materials. The diameter of the shank is described as the gauge and varies between No.2 gauge at the small end of the scale and No.14 at the large end; the length may vary between the very small 6mm or ¼in No.2 to the massive 150mm or 6in No.14. Heads come as countersunk, raised head and roundhead, with either slotted or crosshead tops, and the material of which they are made may be steel, brass, silicon bronze, stainless steel, bright zinc-plated or black japanned. When ordering screws you must state the length, gauge, head and material.

Screws are used where a greater holding power is required than that afforded by nails; where the pieces being joined may have to be taken apart again; or where the vibration associated with nailing would be detrimental. In situations where they may have to be withdrawn from time to time, countersunk screws can be supplied with a cup or socket which fits accurately just under the head. Holes are almost invariably bored for screws, mainly because it is undesirable to have the top part of the screw fitting tightly into the upper piece of wood since this may prevent the joint from closing perfectly. The best policy is to drill the top piece of wood with a hole of a slightly larger diameter than the shank of the screw and pilot drill the under piece with a hole of diameter equal to half the shank diameter in softwood and two-thirds of it in hardwood.

COUNTERSINKING

There are two types of countersinking, the first, shallow countersink, is simply to allow the screw head to lie flat with the surface of the wood and is used in rough work or in places where the screw will not show. The second, much deeper countersink, is used, either so that a screw of shorter length may be used or where the head of the screw will be concealed by a plug.

Plugging
Plugs are used in situations where a screw is the most convenient method of fixing but it is undesirable for the screw to show. In this case the screw is deep countersunk and a plug is glued in the hole, this plug being cut from the same timber and with the grain running in the same direction as the wood being filled. The plug needs to be a perfect fit in the hole and the hole to be perfectly drilled. The best way to obtain perfect results is use a tungsten-tipped plug cutter and to bore the countersink hole with an electric router. If these are not available, drill the hole with a sharp wood

bit and chisel the plug to shape slightly tapered. Hammer the plug firmly home, leaving it proud of the surface so that it can be cleaned level when the glue is dry.

ECCENTRIC SCREWING

It is sometimes desirable to impart a little sideways pull as well as a direct squeezing together, as in the case of the joint shown below. This can be done by boring the small hole in the under piece of wood out-of-centre in relation to the upper piece; the screw then tends to pull the holes so that they are concentric.

SCREWDRIVERS

It is not necessary to have a different size of screwdriver for every size of screw head, but

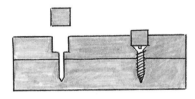

plugging:
the plug is best cut with a tungsten-tipped plug cutter

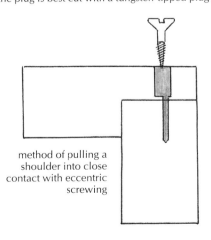

method of pulling a shoulder into close contact with eccentric screwing

Screw plug and eccentric screwing.

a number of sizes are required, perhaps three sizes of conventional screwdriver for slot-head screws and the same for cross-head. The width of the screwdriver blade should be the same as the diameter of the screw head, or at least not far short of it, and it should fit snugly in the slot. If the blade is too short more power than is actually necessary will be needed to turn the screw, and if it is too wide it will mark the wood when the screw is almost home. It is as important to have the blade of your screwdriver kept the right shape and undamaged as it is to keep your chisels sharp. The bottom of the blade must be flat and not rounded in any way, even at the ends, and the sides should likewise be flat tapered and not rounded. When using the screwdriver it is vitally important to maintain pressure on it to keep its position in the slot; if the pressure is relaxed the screwdriver may lift and turn out, causing damage to the screw head and possibly to the work itself.

It is a good idea to have a short, stubby screwdriver in your collection for getting into tight, confined places; but remember that the longer the handle the more power can be exerted and the easier it is to turn the screw.

REMOVING SCREWS

If screws have to be removed for any reason it is, of course, doubly important that the slots have been kept in good condition. Sometimes it may be difficult to get the screw to start turning, especially if it has been in place for some time, and just applying more force may cause the head to break, making extraction even more difficult. If difficulty is experienced a good sharp rap with a hammer on the head of the screwdriver when it is in place on the screw will often do the trick. If not, try tightening the screw a little first; this may sound strange, but it often works. If the screw is still proving stubborn it may be necessary to apply heat to it by holding an electric soldering iron against the head. If after all this effort the worst happens and the head breaks you will need to drill a small hole into the end of the screw and use a screw extractor.

BOLTS

The coachbolt is probably the one most commonly used in woodwork. It consists of a long shank with a thread at one end and a domed head at the other, under which is a square section of shank that is driven into the wood and prevents the bolt from turning when the nut is being tightened. Other bolts are available with slotted screw heads or hexagonal or square bolt heads. The nuts usually have their edges slightly rounded on one side. Where the nuts are not going to be seen it is better to have the rounded side next to the work because this give an easier turning movement. Where the nuts will be seen the rounded side is preferably placed outermost to give a better appearance and be more convenient for passing traffic such as dusters.

METAL FIXING PLATES

Metal fixing plates are manufactured from aluminium, brass or mild steel, and are designed to hold together and strengthen joints or to hold fixtures in place.

GLASS PLATES

Sometimes known as mirror plates, these are available in a range of sizes. They are most often used for securing cabinets and mirror frames to walls. They have a rectangular section that is screwed to the cabinet and a protruding rounded section that is countersunk on the opposite side so as to be fixed to the wall.

Metal fixing plates.

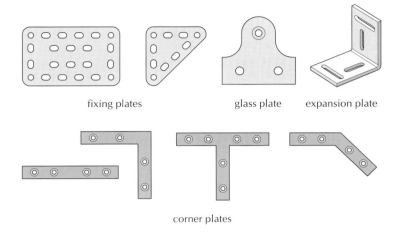

fixing plates   glass plate   expansion plate

corner plates

EXPANSION PLATES

Expansion plates are used for fixing together sections of timber which are likely to shrink. The screw holes in the plates are slotted to allow for movement and they are most often seen securing table- and desk-tops to their underframes.

CORNER PLATES

These come in a variety of shapes, ranging from the actual corner plate to the T-plate, straight mending plate and the angled plate. To use, they are simply screwed in place over the joint to be strengthened. Some of the plates have countersunk holes; if not, roundhead screws may be used.

STRAPS AND HANGERS

A range of these metal fittings are available. They are used to locate and hold structural timbers, the most common of which is the joist hanger.

RAWLPLUGS AND FITTINGS

Much woodwork, especially carpentry, is intended to be secured to a wall, and the method of fixing will depend upon the structure of the wall. In the fairly recent past wood and lead were the only materials from which plugs were made, but now a variety of plastic plugs and metal fittings are available. Plastic plugs are used almost exclusively for fixing into masonry, both interior and exterior. They can be purchased as individual items or as a length of tubing. Some plugs are colour-coded according to their size: yellow, 6–8 gauge,

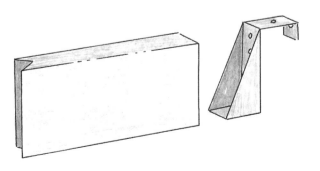

Joist hanger.

5mm drill; red, 8–10 gauge, 6mm drill; brown, 10–14 gauge, 7mm drill, and blue, 14–16 gauge, 10mm drill.

When marking out the position for a rawlplug the screw holes must first be drilled in the item being fixed to the wall. The item is then held to the wall and the position of the holes marked with a pencil passed through the hole. It is important when doing this to ensure with the aid of a spirit level that the item is level. If the item is heavy, this process will either have to be a two-man operation or the item will have to be supported temporarily on a trestle or other structure while the marking of the holes takes place. It is important to clean all the dust out of the hole before inserting the plastic plug, which should be a tight push fit.

WOODEN PLUGS

Wooden plugs are used in the vertical and horizontal joints of brickwork. The mortar in the joint is first cleaned out with a seaming chisel and then the plug is cut to shape with an axe or chisel and hammered into the joint. Care must be taken when using this type of plug near the top or end of a wall not to force the bricks apart and thus form a crack.

COMBINED PLUG AND SCREW FITTING

Some plugs come as a unit complete with a screw. These are designed so that the item being fixed to the wall may be drilled in the one operation, thus eliminating the need to take the item down and offer it up to the wall again.

PLASTERBOARD FITTINGS

Plasterboard fittings come in either metal or plastic and are essentially a threaded plug designed to be screwed into the plaster like a fat screw. The plastic ones come with a special driver, whereas the metal ones are designed to take a standard crosshead screwdriver.

CAVITY FIXINGS

SPRING TOGGLES

The spring toggle is a finely machined nut and bolt with a pair of steel spring-loaded wings which open out on each side. It is used on hollow forms of construction, such as plasterboard walls and plywood and hardboard doors. To use it, a hole must be drilled in the wall that is just large enough to receive the screw, with the spring-loaded wings folded flat to the sides of the screw. The screw is then undone, passed through the item being fixed, and then threaded back on to the nut and wings. The screw is left undone to its furthest extent possible without the risk of the nut's coming off the end. The whole assembly is then offered up to the wall and the spring toggle passed through the hole in the wall, after which the action of turning the screw will pull the nut and the now open wings against the inside of the cavity.

GRAVITY TOGGLES

Gravity toggles are used in exactly the same way as spring toggles; the only difference between them being that the former are not spring-loaded.

EXPANSION ANCHORS

An expansion anchor looks rather like a woodscrew that has already been inserted into a rawlplug. After the anchor piece has been passed through the wall, the action of turning the screw pulls it back on itself until it grips the inside of the panel tightly.

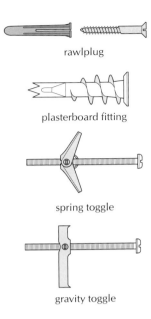

rawlplug

plasterboard fitting

spring toggle

gravity toggle

Cavity fixings.

CRAMPING

It is important when assembling any item of woodwork, whether it is a cabinet, a door or a window frame, to ensure that the piece is held together square while the glue dries. This is accomplished by the use of cramps, and it is necessary to have some understanding of their proper use otherwise it is possible to pull the work out of square and spoil a perfectly good job.

There are several different types of cramp available, but the sash cramp and the G-cramp are the two most common, and certain aspects are common to both. Both will mark the wood if they are used without some kind of protection between the pad of the cramp and the work itself; so always make sure that some off-cuts of timber are available. These may either be secured to the pad of the cramp itself or held in place on the work with masking tape in the appropriate position. Use soft-

wood for all pads; hardwoods may cause as much damage as the cramp itself.

Both the sash and the G-cramp are capable of exerting a great deal of pressure; but this should not be necessary: if a lot of force is needed to pull a joint together then something is wrong somewhere. Check that there is nothing in the joint preventing it from going together, check that the air and any excess of glue are able to escape, and check that the tenon has not been left too long for the mortise; remember that it will need some space at the bottom.

When positioning a cramp on the work, remember that the line of force is between the centres of the pads at either end of the cramp. Make sure that these centres are in line with the centre of the joint; any failure to do so could pull the joint out of line.

Give thought to the order of assembly; it may be that the side frames need to be glued together first; do not be tempted to try to assemble the whole structure in one operation since this is seldom a good idea. Sometimes it is necessary to apply a cramp to a surface that is angled or shaped and it turns out that the cramp will not naturally stay in the correct place for cramping. This is often the case with chairs, and under these circumstances the worker has two options: it is possible when cutting out a shaped piece that has a joint in it to leave a square section where the cramp will go, and to shape and clean this part up after it has been assembled. If this is not practicable for one reason

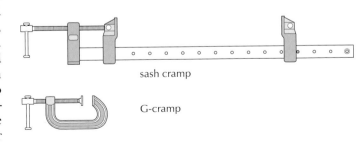

sash cramp

G-cramp

Sash and G-cramps.

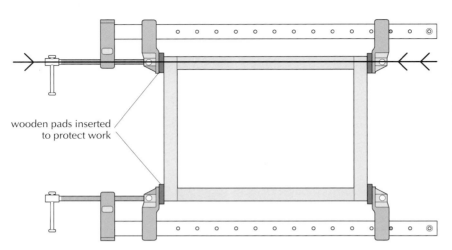

Sash cramps in use.

the line of force is between the centre of the pads and must be kept in line with the centre of the joint

wooden pads inserted to protect work

or another, then a shaped block can be cut to fit and held in place temporarily for cramping. It will usually be necessary to cut and shape the block so that it has a section that allows the block itself to be cramped in place to prevent slipping.

It is possible to pull a frame out of shape when cramping and it is important always to check for square after the cramp has been tightened. It is possible to correct small amounts of misalignment by repositioning the cramp. If, for instance, you

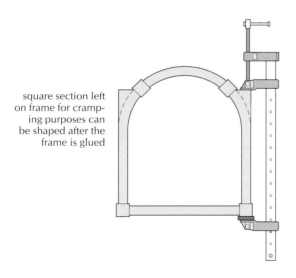

square section left on frame for cramping purposes can be shaped after the frame is glued

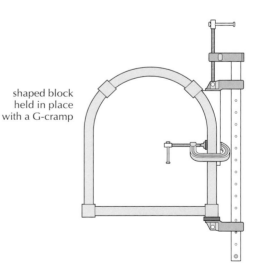

shaped block held in place with a G-cramp

Cramping a curved surface.

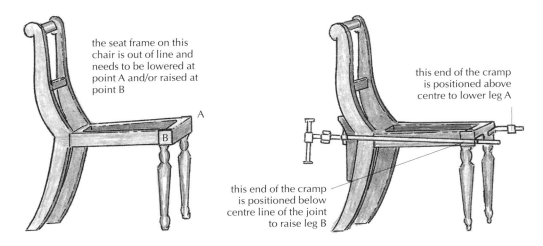

the seat frame on this chair is out of line and needs to be lowered at point A and/or raised at point B

this end of the cramp is positioned above centre to lower leg A

this end of the cramp is positioned below centre line of the joint to raise leg B

Correcting misalignment.

have just cramped together a chair and the seat frame is out of line, as shown, lowering one end of one cramp and raising the end of the other will pull the seat into line. Usually only a small adjustment is needed.

SASH CRAMPS

Sash cramps are useful for assembling square frameworks; they come in various lengths, and are either flat or T-section.

The latter is by far the stronger of the two and will not bend in use; but the flat section is more versatile, inasmuch as it is possible to join two together for cramping long sections of work. To join two flat section cramps together, the adjustable ends are removed and the two sections are cramped together with small G-cramps. This must be done with the holes of each cramp lined up so that the pegs can be placed through the holes to prevent any

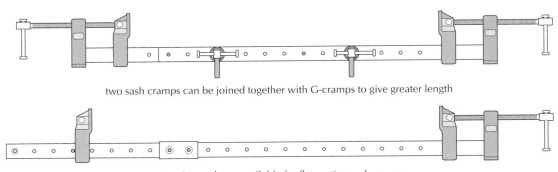

two sash cramps can be joined together with G-cramps to give greater length

extension ends are available for flat section sash cramps

Extending the length of a sash cramp.

slipping. It is possible to purchase special extension ends for these cramps instead of joining two together. It is also possible to purchase cramp ends only, which are then fitted to a length of batten that can be cut to any length.

G-CRAMPS

G-cramps may be used for a great variety of cramping jobs, including veneering, splicing and holding wood temporarily for screwing. They come in many sizes and it is worth having a good selection of them.

QUICK-ACTION CRAMPS

These also come in a variety of sizes which may be used in place of sash or G-cramps. Some even have an action like that of a mastic gun that allows you to fit the cramp single-handedly. This may be useful when you need another hand to hold something in place for it to be cramped.

WEBBING CRAMPS

Webbing cramps are particularly useful for shaped work and for holding the headrails on some designs of chair.

CHAIR CRAMPS

Chair cramps are some of the most versatile of cramps; they can often be used in place of sash cramps and have the advantage of a quick action and a deep throat, which means that they are capable of reaching parts that a sash cramp could not.

MASKING TAPE

Good quality masking tape may not spring to mind when one considers cramps, but there are circumstances, especially with small, shaped objects when it is invaluable. Use it double for extra strength.

RUBBER BANDS

An old car tyre inner tube can be cut into rubber bands which are useful for holding small, delicate or awkwardly shaped items.

UPHOLSTERY SPRINGS

Old upholstery coil springs may be cut as shown below and used as small but very effective cramps for delicate work.

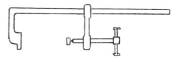

quick action cramp

upholstery spring

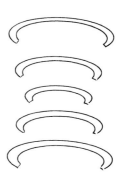

upholstery spring cut to
make small spring cramps

Old coil springs can be used as cramps.

10

Chamfering, Bevelling and Rounding

CHAMFERING

Chamfering is the removal of wood from an edge to form a narrow flat, often at 45 degrees to the surface. It is done either to improve the appearance of the work or to diminish the risk of damage to sharp corners. On rough work neither the exact angle nor the width of the chamfer is taken into account. On straight edges the chamfer is achieved with the use of a jack or smoothing plane, whereas on curved edges a spokeshave or file is employed.

The chamfer may run all the way around an outer edge, but it is more frequently used on the inner edges of panelled framework, and, in this case, the chamfers are invariably stopped before they reach a corner. The two most common forms of stop are shown in *A* and *B* below, but more elaborate forms may also be used on ornate pieces (*see C* and *D*).

When marking out a chamfer it is advisable to use a pencil rather than a marking gauge, because chamfering will not easily remove the marks made by the gauge. The stops are formed with a chisel, used flat to produce the flat stop and in the reverse way to produce the curved stop.

An electric router may be used to make chamfers and the cutter will automatically form its own stop; however, the drawback to the use of the router is the fact that its high speed will often cause burning along the edge of the work where the stylus runs.

BEVELLING

Bevelling is the planing of surfaces which are not at right angles; a chamfer, of course, is an example of this but it is not called a bevel because it is merely an

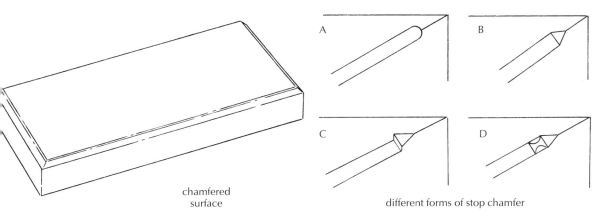

chamfered
surface

different forms of stop chamfer

Chamfered edges.

ornamental detail. A bevel is usually of equal importance to other main surfaces of the work: it may be necessary in forming a joint or the shape of the work may require it. It may be at an angle of 45 degrees, which in some circumstances will be called a mitre, or it may be at any other angle.

ROUNDING

Edges may be rounded instead of chamfered, and this may be anything from a small round, which can be achieved with the use of sandpaper alone, or a larger curve which requires accurate marking out and planing. Rounding is usually carried out with flat cutters, for example, a plane, spokeshave or chisel. Because of this they will require more sanding than a flat surface does since the curve will in reality be a series of narrow flats, the ridges of which will have to be sanded. This will not, however, be the case if the round was made with an electric router and the appropriate cutter. There is a great variety in the form a rounded edge may take, as may be seen from the illustrations below.

Occasionally a comparatively large outside radius is required where there is only a

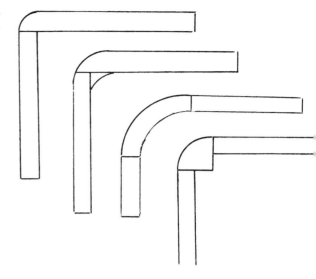

Four methods of building up a large radius.

limited thickness of material and thus some building up will be required. Four methods of building up a corner are shown above, and the choice made will depend upon the radius of the required curve and whether the interior is also required to be curved.

Very large curves cannot be successfully cut from the solid as this would invariably

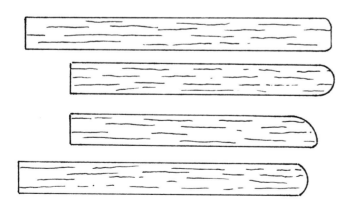

There is great variety in the form a rounded edge may take.

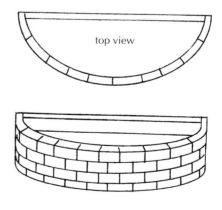

top view

Curve built up of rows of small overlapping blocks.

70

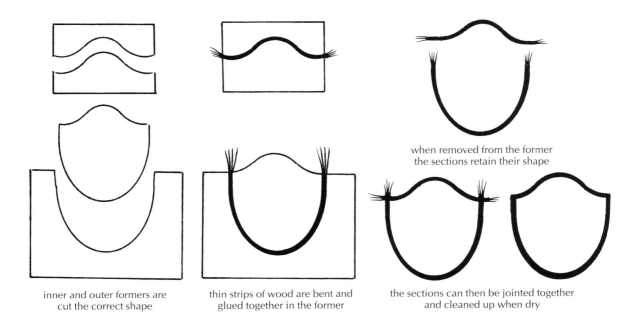

when removed from the former
the sections retain their shape

inner and outer formers are
cut the correct shape

thin strips of wood are bent and
glued together in the former

the sections can then be jointed together
and cleaned up when dry

Laminating a frame.

mean that there would be areas of short grain and the structure would be weakened. There are two ways to overcome this problem. First, it is possible to build up the bend with rows of small overlapping timber, rather like brickwork. The required shape is drawn full-size on a plywood base and a plywood template is made for checking the structure as it builds up. The first row is positioned over the drawing, making sure that the joints between them are close. The template is then used to draw the curve on these blocks and the second row is glued in place on top of them. This process is repeated until the structure is complete. When it is dry the inner and the outer surface are finally shaped with a plane and veneered if required.

The second method is to laminate or build up the required curve in layers. If we take as an example the shield-shaped frame shown above, inner and outer formers of the correct shape are cut from strong, solid timber or some other material. Strips of wood are then cut which are thin enough to be bent to the required shape. In the case of the bottom bend in our shield it is possible that even these thin strips will require some steaming. The strips are cut slightly wider than required to allow for some cleaning up after the glue has dried, and the outermost strip may, of course, be a decorative veneer. The strips of wood are glued together and placed between the two halves of the former. The former is then cramped together with G-cramps, starting in the middle, working out towards the ends and cleaning off any excess of glue. To prevent the strips of wood from adhering to the former itself it is advisable to oil the inside edges and even to put a layer of paper between the edge of the former and the wood strips.

11

Joints

REBATING

The terms, rebate, rabbet and rabbit all mean the same thing, but rebate is probably the original and more correct word. The rebate is used in the formation of joints and is cut usually across the grain on the end of a board in order to receive the

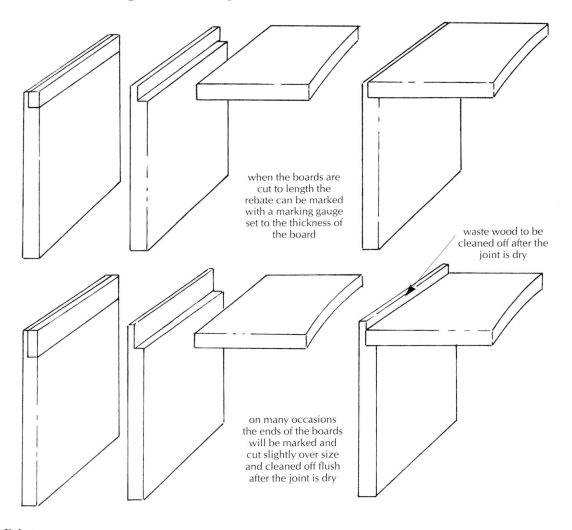

when the boards are cut to length the rebate can be marked with a marking gauge set to the thickness of the board

waste wood to be cleaned off after the joint is dry

on many occasions the ends of the boards will be marked and cut slightly over size and cleaned off flush after the joint is dry

Rebates.

end of another, normally at right angles. The advantage of the rebate over the butt joint in this situation is that it can be nailed from both directions and will keep the end of the work flush, when a butt joint could easily be forced out of position.

When marking out the rebate it is usual, if the ends of the board are cut to length, to use a marking gauge set to the thickness of the other board. On many occasions, however, the ends of the board will be marked and cut slightly over size and so the rebate will have to be marked with a square. The waste wood is cleaned off flush, after the joint is dry.

In rough work it is possible to cut to the lines with the saw; however, if a better appearance is required for the finished work it is advisable to cut near to the line and then use a rebate plane or chisel to finish off accurately. When cutting a rebate in line with the grain a saw cut is not necessary as the rebate may be cut with a plough plane or router.

Rebates are often used in a framework to accept glass or other panels that may at some time need to be changed, and on these occasions the panel is normally held in place with a small bead or putty. When making up a rebated frame in this manner it is usual to use a long and short shoulder tenon.

GROOVING AND HOUSING

A groove is simply a rebate that is not at the end of a board and therefore has two shoulders instead of one. There are two types, the first is used for joining two pieces of similar thickness at right angles, as is the case when fitting the ends of shelves into uprights, and this type is generally called a housing joint. The second is mainly found in the edges of boards, cut to receive thin tongues, as with tongued and grooved floorboards or the chamfered edges of panels. This second type is usually cut with a plough plane; the first type is a little more complicated. Because a groove has two shoulders it is not possible to use a rebate or shoulder plane for cleaning up, and if it is not cut to the line with the saw the shoulders will have to be cleaned up with a chisel.

There are some variations possible with the groove or housing joint, and these take the form of the reduced width groove, as shown overleaf, which is useful near the end of a board if a full-width groove would leave very short and consequently weak end grain. Another variation is the dovetailed groove, which prevents the pieces from pulling directly apart. Dovetailed grooves or 'slot dovetails' may be one- or two-sided and have to be slid in and out. Slot dovetails are troublesome to cut and are used only on work of a superior quality when the additional security is desirable. They are first cut exactly as an ordinary groove to the width of the narrowest part and then undercut with a chisel to the extent of the vee (*see* the later description of the slot dovetail on page 88).

EDGE JOINTS

When boards have to be joined flat along their edges to increase the width, as in the making of a tabletop, for instance, there are several possible methods. With each of them it is first necessary to ensure that the edges meet together along their full length without gaps and that the two pieces lie perfectly flat. To achieve this, the boards must be planed together. Decide which sides are to be the top surfaces and which edges are to be joined and plane the edges straight so that they are a reasonable fit together. Place the pieces to be joined on a flat surface with the edges together and the faces uppermost. Now turn one over on

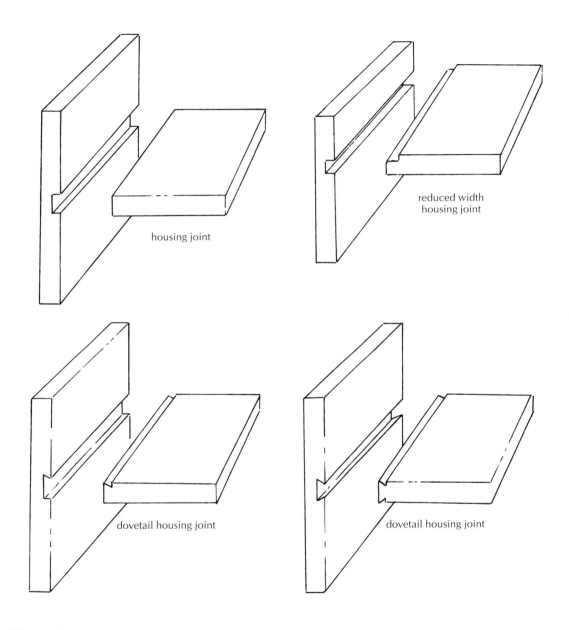

housing joint

reduced width
housing joint

dovetail housing joint

dovetail housing joint

Housing joints.

top of the other, as if you were closing a book, and get the edges as flush as possible and secure them in the position with small G-cramps. Place them in a vice and plane the two edges perfectly straight with a try-plane. By planing the two pieces together in this way it does not matter so much if the edges are not quite square with the surface because when they are opened out again they will still lie flat.

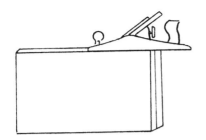

the edges to be joined are planed together

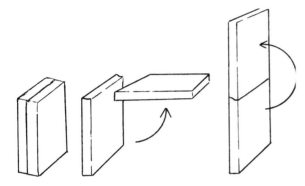

even if the edges have not been planed exactly square
the two pieces will be in line when opened out

Edge joints.

Having said that, I do not want to give the impression that it would be acceptable to plane the edges at a definite angle to the surface; the squarer the better when it comes to their assembly. This method, however, eliminates the need for perfect squareness and you can concentrate your efforts on getting the edges straight. To test, hold one piece upright in the vice with the planed edge uppermost and rest the other piece on it. It should be possible to feel whether the two pieces are fitting perfectly by gently trying to rock and swivel the top piece; if they are fitting well you should be able to feel some resistance to this action.

RUBBED JOINT

It is possible at this stage to joint the pieces together with glue alone. The glue is applied to both edges and they are, quite literally, rubbed back and forth together; when the movement feels stiff bring them to their final alignment and cramp in place, cleaning off any excess of glue. It is good practice to cramp straight pieces of timber, about 50mm (2in) thick, across the work, both above and below to prevent bowing when the cramps are tightened. Small pads of wood must be placed between the work and the cramp so that the metal is not in contact with the wood since there is a possibility that any glue squeezing out of the joint, underneath the cramp, will react with the metal and stain the work.

DOWELLED JOINT

It is possible to add some strength to the edge joint by the addition of dowels. The position of the dowels has to be accurately marked, and this is best achieved by the use of a dowelling jig. This is easily made from plywood cut to size, with pins driven through in the place of the dowels. The jig is held in place on the edge of the work and then tapped with a hammer so that the nails mark the position of the dowels. Drill a small pilot hole first before drilling to the correct size in order to reduce the chance of the drill's wandering. An alternative to this is simply to drive pins into one edge, leaving them proud and then snipping off the heads. The two pieces may then be lined up, brought together and lightly cramped, driving the cut off ends of the pins into the other side of the joint. Separate the two halves and remove the pins with the aid of a pair of pincers.

When dowelling always cut the dowel a little short to allow for any excess of glue which will be pushed to the bottom of the

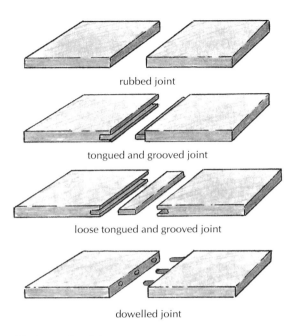

rubbed joint

tongued and grooved joint

loose tongued and grooved joint

dowelled joint

Various edge joints.

dowel hole, and always chamfer the end of the dowel and cut grooves in the side to allow air and glue to escape.

TONGUED AND GROOVED JOINT

The tongued and grooved joint is strong but has the disadvantage of being visible on the ends, unless some form of moulding or capping is being applied. In practice, it is also difficult to obtain a perfect fit with both shoulders. The tongue should be one-third of the thickness of the board and slightly short of the full depth of the groove to allow the best possible fit of the shoulders.

LOOSE TONGUED AND GROOVED JOINT

This joint has the advantage of giving a good glue line because it is prepared in the same way as a rubbed joint. The tongue or spline is still one-third of the thickness of the board and should be of a hard wood. This joint is particularly good for jointing chipboard because any tongue cut in chipboard itself would be too fragile.

SLOT-SCREWED JOINT

Prepare as for a rubbed joint and mark the position of the screws. Drill a hole the diameter of the screw head to one side of the mark and cut a slot the width of the screw shank from the hole just past the position of the screw. Insert the screws in the other edge, apply glue and bring the surfaces together, inserting the screw heads in the holes, hold together firmly and knock the one plank sideways so that the screw heads bite into the slot. I am not a fan of this type of joint, but it does have the advantage that it is held relatively firmly without a cramp and this could be helpful under some circumstances.

HALVED AND LAPPED JOINTS

The basic half-lap joint is one of the easiest to execute and can be used for lengthening rails and posts, or, in the case of the corner half lap, for simple framework. The terms halved and lapped are often used interchangeably, but while a half joint is always a lapped one, a lapped joint does not have to be halved. There are four half-lap joints: the straight half lap, the corner half lap, the tee half lap, and the cross half lap.

Mark the lines square on the face side, the width of the joint, continue these lines on to the face edges with a try square (remember: stock and faces go together). Set a gauge to half the thickness of the timber and scribe lines, again working from the face side, along the side, up to

Cutting a lapped joint.

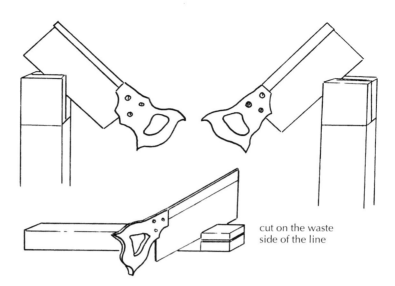

cut on the waste
side of the line

the end and across the end grain. After marking out, set one of the rails in the vice, on end, and begin cutting with a tenon saw. Cut on the waste side of the line, starting at the corner and working down the side facing you and along the end grain, cutting only what you can see. Turn the rail around and repeat on the other side, then cut straight across and down to the shoulder line. Placing the rail either in the vice or on a bench hook, cut the shoulder. Any cleaning up of the joint is done with a paring chisel, after which the joint may be glued and pinned.

The process just described differs only when it comes to cutting out the section of timber between the shoulders of the cross and tee half-joint. In these cases the shoulders are cut down to the scribe line, first from one side and then from the other, as normal. Extra cuts are then made in the waste wood, down to the scribe line. The waste wood is next removed with a chisel: place the chisel against the side of the waste and tap with a mallet, taking a small amount of wood at a time, gradually working down to the scribe line, but not going all the way across to the other side because this could cause the wood to split out. Turn

the rail around and repeat, again working down to the line in stages and not going all the way across. Finally, clean the bottom of the joint flat with the chisel and check for flatness with the blade of a try square. Remember: mark each half of the joint exactly and cut on the waste side of the line; it is better to have the joint too tight rather than too loose, as the former can be remedied.

BEVELLED HALF LAP

Another variation of the half lap is the bevelled half lap as shown overleaf; it is cut in the same way, but the depth of the joint cannot be marked with a gauge and a piece of tapered wood is used as a template.

DOVETAIL HALF LAP

The dovetail half lap may be regarded as a modified tee half lap and is used a great deal in cabinet making. The pin part is made first in the same way as for an ordinary lap joint and then the shoulders are sawn to the required angle. The pin half is then held over the piece for the socket and the socket is marked from it. The shoulders of the socket are squared down and then cut with a tenon saw, the waste wood being removed with a chisel.

THE MORTISE AND TENON

The mortise and tenon joint is the strongest method of joining one piece of wood to another and has a number of different forms. First we shall look at the simple 'closed' mortise and tenon, so called because it has wood on all four sides, and then at other variations.

CLOSED MORTISE AND TENON

In marking out a mortise and tenon joint it is usual for the thickness of the mortise to be one-third of the width of the timber, or

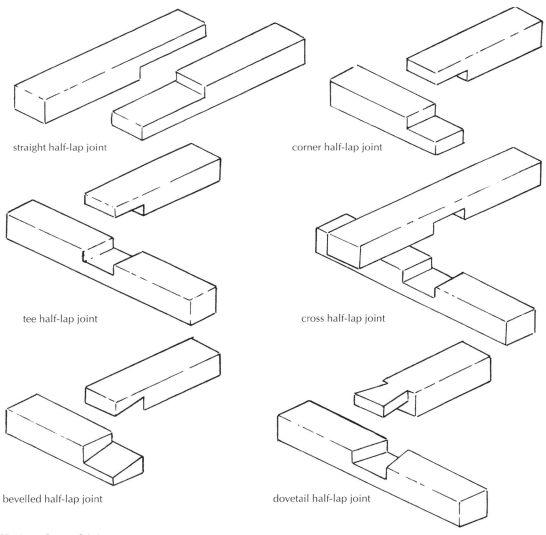

straight half-lap joint

corner half-lap joint

tee half-lap joint

cross half-lap joint

bevelled half-lap joint

dovetail half-lap joint

Various lapped joints.

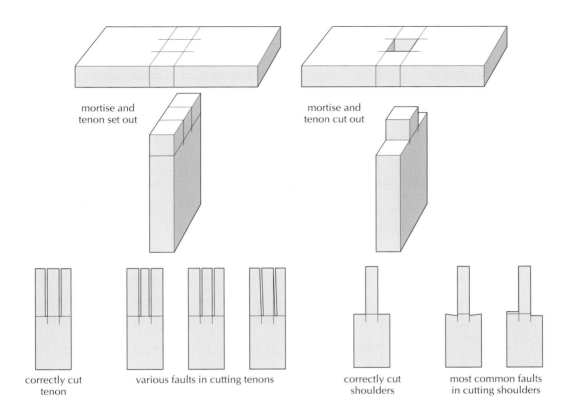

mortise and tenon set out

mortise and tenon cut out

correctly cut tenon

various faults in cutting tenons

correctly cut shoulders

most common faults in cutting shoulders

Mortise and tenon.

as near to one-third as you have a chisel for. The width of the tenon should be no more than four times the thickness; if it is more than this shrinkage could leave the tenon slack. It is usual to set a mortise gauge for marking out, and this must be used with the stock against the face side for both mortise and tenon.

Cutting the Mortise

The mortise is cut first, and much time may be saved if the bulk of the waste timber is removed by boring before you begin with the chisel. Boring to the required depth also acts as a handy depth gauge if the tenon does not go all the way through. Once two or three holes have been bored to the correct depth, the chisel is held upright in the

middle of the mortise and struck with a mallet. Push the chisel away from you and remove, repeat this action a little closer to you each time until you almost reach the end line, turn the chisel around and repeat in the opposite direction. Clear out the waste and repeat, this time a little deeper until the bottom of the tenon is reached and then finally, holding the chisel upright, clean up to the end lines.

Sawing the Tenon

When sawing the tenon the rail is held in the vice, upright, or almost so, and the cut is started on the waste side at one corner. Start off by putting your thumbnail neatly on the line to act as a guide for the first couple of saw strokes. Begin with one or two back strokes first because there is always a danger that the saw will jump if you begin with forward strokes and this could damage either yourself or the work. Continue cutting down the side of the tenon nearest to you and along the end of the rail; do not at this stage cut down the line on the other side of the rail that you cannot see. Reverse the rail and repeat the operation on the other side. Now, with the saw straight across the end of the rail, continue the cut down to the shoulder line. When cutting the shoulder the cut is started with the point down, the handle being slowly lowered until the saw is horizontal; the cutting is continued until the tenon cut is met and the 'cheek' drops off. The most common faults in cutting tenons are shown in the illustration on the previous page.

SLOT MORTISE AND TENON

In this joint, also known as an open mortise and tenon, the mortise is merely a slot cut in the end of the rail so that the tenon can be inserted from the side.

BRIDLE JOINT

The bridle joint is really a slot mortise, but, instead of having a tenon fitting into it, a rail is housed out on either side and sits across the top. The bridle joint is useful for the centre leg of a settee or table.

HAUNCHED MORTISE AND TENON

In the cases where the mortised timber has to be cut level with the rail, as with most doors, and a slot mortise and tenon is impracticable, a haunched mortise and tenon is used. In this joint the mortise is made shorter than the width of the tenon, and the tenon is cut away as shown. The tenon is first cut full-size, as for an ordinary tenon, and then the haunch is marked and the small piece of waste cut away. The recess for the haunch is marked on the end of the mortised rail and is sawn with the end of the tenon saw down to the lines, when the waste is then removed with a chisel. Another form of this joint is the secret haunched mortise and tenon, as shown; in this joint the haunch is not visible on the end of the rail.

THROUGH MORTISE AND TENON

The through mortise and tenon is as the name implies, it is a mortise and tenon joint in which the tenon goes right through the rail rather than only three-quarters of the way in. It is usual for this type of joint to be wedged from the other side, and the mortise is cut slightly longer on that side to accommodate it. The through tenon may be of the ordinary or haunched form and both forms can be wedged if desired.

BAREFACED TENON

A barefaced tenon is one that has only one shoulder, the other side being flush with the face. It can be used in situations where the rail is thin and a shoulder each side would put the mortise too near the edge of the rail.

TUSK TENON

The tusk tenon is made long enough to project on the far side and has a hole cut in it to receive a tapered key or peg. It is most commonly used for framing or floor joists and, in a somewhat simpler form, for the cross rails of refectory tables. With the tusk mortise and tenon that is used for floor joists the mortise is not positioned in the middle of the joist for reasons of strength. The underside of the tenon is positioned on the middle line of the joist so that the whole of the tenon is situated in the top or compression half of the joist. If the tenon

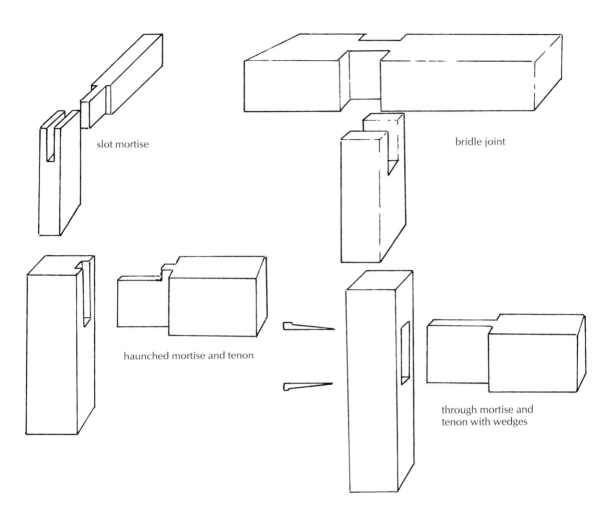

slot mortise

bridle joint

haunched mortise and tenon

through mortise and
tenon with wedges

Various mortise and tenon joints.

were positioned in the bottom or tension half of the joist it would be more likely to break down.

DOUBLE TENONS

In the case of wide timbers, such as the backs of side tables and desks or the bottom and middle rails of panel doors, a double tenon is employed. This is done both to avoid excessive shrinkage which could take place causing the tenons to become slack,

and to avoid any weakening of the rail with such a large mortise. These tenons are haunched in order to stop the rail's warping and also to prevent light from coming, through should the joint open at all. It is a good idea to limit the width of the tenons to no more than six times its thickness.

A different kind of double tenon is required with wide rails, as may be seen with the front seat rail of a regency chair (*see* overleaf); notice that the rear tenon is shorter in length than the front one.

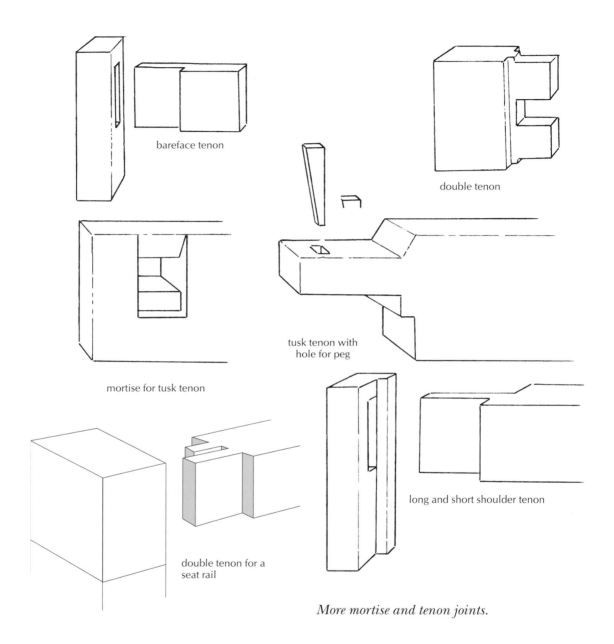

bareface tenon

double tenon

mortise for tusk tenon

tusk tenon with
hole for peg

double tenon for a
seat rail

long and short shoulder tenon

More mortise and tenon joints.

LONG AND SHORT SHOULDER TENON

The long and short shoulder tenon is used when the rails have been rebated, the long shoulder making up for the depth of the rebate, as shown. In marking out this joint it is usual to have one side of the mortise against the inside of the rebate for ease of cutting.

MITRED TENON

The mitred tenon is used in situations where it is desirable to have a mitre showing rather than a square shoulder on the face of the work; this is normal in the case of picture frames, for example. The tenon is marked out and cut as usual, except for the fact that the shoulders are cut at 45 degrees rather than square. This can be the case for both shoulders or just the front one.

PEGS

Early mortise and tenon joints, such as those found on oak furniture of the sixteenth and the seventeenth century, were pegged. That is to say, that they had a piece of timber of square section, with the edges

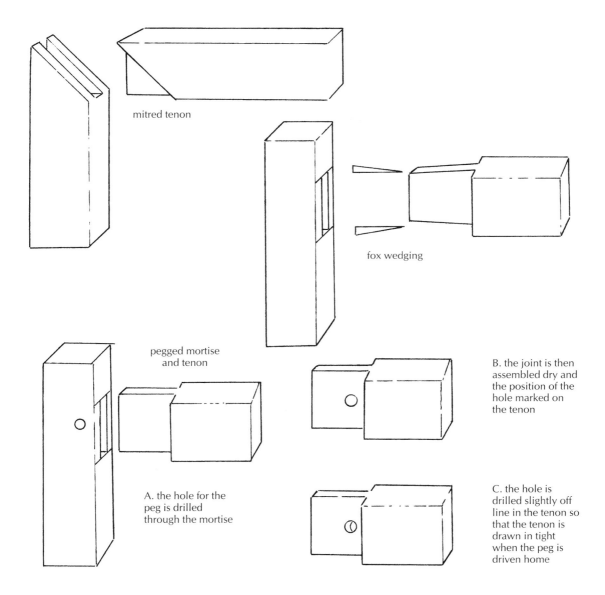

mitred tenon

fox wedging

pegged mortise and tenon

A. the hole for the peg is drilled through the mortise

B. the joint is then assembled dry and the position of the hole marked on the tenon

C. the hole is drilled slightly off line in the tenon so that the tenon is drawn in tight when the peg is driven home

Pegged and wedged tenons.

pared down and slightly tapered, driven through the mortise from the outside of the rail in order to hold the tenon in place. The joint is marked out and cut in the usual way and a hole drilled through the mortise so that it will pass through the tenon when the joint is assembled. The joint is then assembled dry and the position of the hole is marked on the side of the tenon, which is then withdrawn. The hole is then drilled in the tenon, but slightly out of line, being drilled a little nearer to the shoulder so that the action of driving home the peg will draw the tenon in, ensuring a tight fit at the shoulders.

FOX WEDGING

It has already been said that through tenons can be given extra security by wedging from the exposed end; but it is also possible to wedge a closed mortise and tenon. In this case the mortise is cut a little wider at the base when chiselling out and the end of the tenon is cut down with a tenon saw to about two-thirds its depth and a little in from each side to receive the wedges, as shown on the previous page. The wedges themselves must be cut to the correct length to fit the cuts in the tenon or they will prevent the tenon's being pulled up tight; but they must not be so thick at the widest part that there is not enough room for the tenon to expand. To assemble, the joint is glued, including the wedges which are tapped just a little way into the end of the tenon before assembly begins. As the joint is driven home, so the wedges are driven in, expanding the end of the tenon.

THE DOVETAIL

ORDINARY OR BOX DOVETAIL

For the purpose of explanation, let us take the case of marking out and cutting the dovetails for a simple, square box. First, of course, the four sides will have been planed, smoothed and the ends shot true. The back and the front of the box are put together face-to-face in the same position as they will occupy when the box is finished, and are held together with small pins, keeping the face edges flush. A marking gauge is set exactly to the thickness of the wood being joined and a line is scribed round the ends of the two sides just joined. Do not scribe the lines too deeply but just enough to be able to see them; remember that they will have to be removed with a cabinet scrape before finishing can start. Decide how many dovetail pins are required, the pins being the wedge-shaped projections that fit into corresponding sockets on the other piece. The fan-shaped sections of wood left between the pins and the sockets are the tails. As a general rule, in hand work the pins are smaller that the tails; in fact, the smaller the pin the finer the work. However, quite often with machine dovetails the pins and the tails are of the same size. Let us assume that our box requires five pins and, as we are making a box of some quality, they will be quite small compared to the size of the tails. We shall be marking and cutting the sockets first. On the end of each side, mark in a distance compatible to the width of one socket and divide the intervening space into as many equal parts, plus one, as there are sockets. Thus for five sockets there will be six equal divisions.

Set a bevel to the correct angle; if you do not have a dovetail template about 10 degrees is usually about right. It is a mistake to have the angle too obtuse, because, although this may look stronger, the wood is cut more across the grain and there is a danger of the pins' splitting out when the joint is put together. From each dividing line mark off half the width of a socket at its narrowest on either side; in the case of some dovetails on fine furniture, the

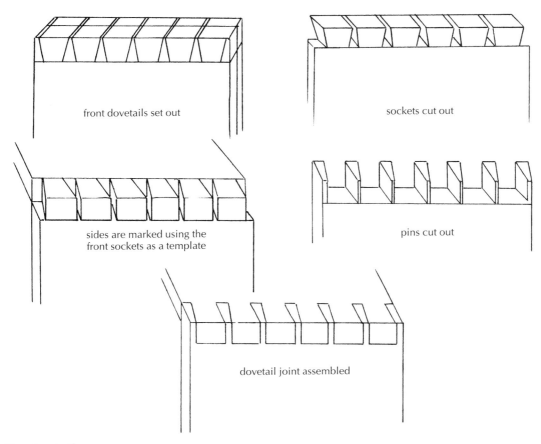

front dovetails set out

sockets cut out

sides are marked using the
front sockets as a template

pins cut out

dovetail joint assembled

Box dovetail.

narrow part of the socket is only as wide as the saw cut, in which case these marks are unnecessary. Mark the inclined lines on one side, square the lines across the end grain and mark the inclined lines again on the other side. Cut down the inclined lines with a tenon or dovetail saw, keeping to the waste side of the line and cutting accurately to the scribed line. The two sides may now be separated and the joining pins removed. One of the other side pieces to be marked is now set upright in the vice with the outer side facing you. One of the pieces just cut is now rested on this at right angles, inside downwards, with the edges

quite flush. It may be necessary to place something on the bench to support the other end and to keep it level.

The pins may now be marked on the end grain, either with a marking knife or by inserting the point of the saw. Before removing them, both pieces must be marked for identification to ensure that these two pieces go together in the final assembly. The pins are now squared down from the marks on the end grain to the scribed line and then cut, once again with a tenon or dovetail saw. Remember to cut on the waste side, which will be on the other side of the line from when you cut

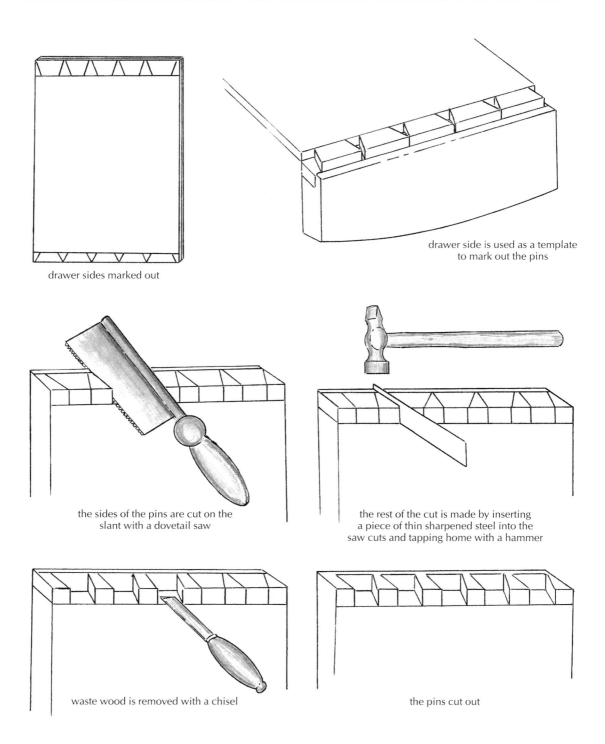

drawer sides marked out

drawer side is used as a template
to mark out the pins

the sides of the pins are cut on the
slant with a dovetail saw

the rest of the cut is made by inserting
a piece of thin sharpened steel into the
saw cuts and tapping home with a hammer

waste wood is removed with a chisel

the pins cut out

Lap dovetail.

the socket. The waste wood of the sockets may now be removed either with a fine chisel or a coping saw. If the latter is used, it is best to keep a little away from the line so that the final cleaning up is done with a chisel in order to keep the edge good and sharp. The sockets at the ends can, of course, be removed with a tenon saw. The waste from between the pins is next cut out in the same way as that from the sockets. If all the cuts have been made accurately, the joint is now ready for assembly and will require only gluing. Once together the box is checked for square by measuring across the diagonals; if they measure the same then the box is square.

LAP DOVETAIL

This is the joint most commonly used for drawer fronts because end grain shows only on the side, not on the front. Normally, when this joint is employed the wood at the front is thicker than that at the side, and the width and the length of the pins are made equal to the thickness of the side. With some antique drawers, however, the sides are very thin and therefore the pins will be longer.

The gauge is set to the thickness of the side and a line is scribed round the end of the sides, which have been pinned together as before. Another line is then scribed along the end of the drawer front, but only on the side that will be the inside of the drawer, and also along the end grain of the drawer front with the stock against the inside of the drawer front. To set out the sockets and pins proceed in the same manner as described earlier for box dovetails. The real difference in making the lap dovetail as opposed to the box dovetail comes in the removing of the waste between the pins, because it is not possible to use a coping saw. The drawer front is placed in the vice with a piece of stout timber behind it, as shown, to prevent the

front from breaking out during hammering. The sides of the pins are cut with a tenon or dovetail saw, but may be cut only on the slant. The rest of the cut is made by inserting a piece of thin sharpened steel, such as the ground end of a hacksaw blade, into the saw cuts and tapping this home with a hammer.

Great care must be taken if the pins are very fine not to break them at their thinnest point. A sharp chisel is then tapped in at the base of the waste, just above the line, as shown; it is then possible to tap the chisel in from the top and to remove a sliver of waste wood. This process is repeated until most of the waste has been removed, at which time it will be possible to clean down to the lines. Do not fall into the trap of undercutting the sides; make sure that you keep them all square, otherwise the finished joint will not be so secure.

DOUBLE LAP DOVETAIL

We have seen that in the lap dovetail the joint does not show from the front, but in the double lap dovetail the joint is 'secret' – not showing from either the front or the side. The front and the side are conveniently of the same size and the pins may be on either.

Set the gauge to the thickness of the wood and scribe a line on the inside at the ends and over at the top and the bottom edges, as shown. Next adjust the gauge to about one-third of the thickness and scribe another line parallel to the first and also on the end edge. The pins are then set out as already described, squared up to the edge. With secret dovetails, the pins and the tails may be equal in size. The pins can now be cut with the saw and the waste removed with a chisel as before, and the joint will appear as shown.

Cuts are then made down the outer lines until they meet so that the rebate is formed. To mark the sockets, adjust the

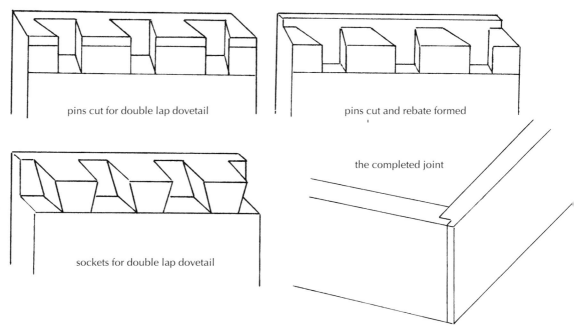

pins cut for double lap dovetail

pins cut and rebate formed

the completed joint

sockets for double lap dovetail

Double lap dovetail.

gauge to two-thirds of the thickness and mark a shoulder line on the end and on the side edges. Then, placing the stock of the gauge against what will be the inside of the piece, mark a line on the end edge. The sockets may now be marked from the pins as before, cut with a saw and the waste removed with a chisel, as for a lap dovetail. When the joint is together the corner is often rounded to give a better appearance.

SECRET MITRED DOVETAIL

If you want a secret dovetail joint but do not want to round the end or have any end grain showing at all then the mitred dovetail is the answer. Proceed with marking and cutting the pins in exactly the same way as for the double lap dovetail. The socket side is then marked out in the same way and the rebate cut but left square at this time. Place the two pieces together, as shown opposite, to mark the sockets from

the pins and proceed to cut the sockets. Now the two projecting laps must be cut to 45 degrees, either by cutting with a chisel or by using a rebate plane. One of the best ways to achieve a good mitre is to cut one on a piece of board and to cramp this to the work as shown, using it as a template to work against. The joint will now appear as shown. The final stage is to continue the lap mitre across the end pins.

SLOT DOVETAIL

The slot dovetail is used as an alternative to a housing joint to prevent any possibility of the cabinet sides' spreading. There are two ways in which this joint can be executed, and three if you count using a dovetail cutter in an electric router (*see* Chapter 16). The first is used if the slot dovetail is extending across the full width of the board. In this case the outline of the dovetail is marked on both sides of the work and

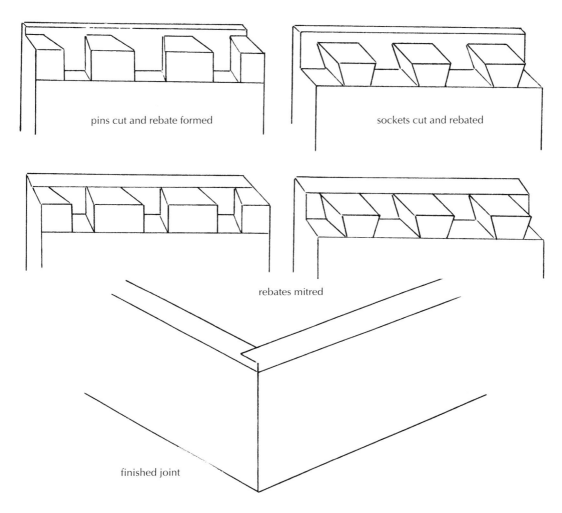

pins cut and rebate formed

sockets cut and rebated

rebates mitred

finished joint

Mitred dovetail.

the line of the shoulders is squared across between them. The dovetail may have a slope on both sides, but it is more usual for just one side to be sloped and the other left square with the face of the board. The dovetail extends the full width of the board and therefore it is possible to cut both the square side and the sloping side with a tenon saw and then to clean out the waste with a chisel. If the dovetail is to stop short of one side of the board, it is not possible to cut right through with a tenon saw. It is more usual under these circumstances to mark and cut both shoulders square initially and then to pare down the sloping side with a paring chisel.

TAPERED SLOT DOVETAIL

The tapered slot dovetail always has a slope on both sides and is most often seen securing the legs of tripod tables or the under-supports of wall brackets. It is best to mark out and cut this joint square

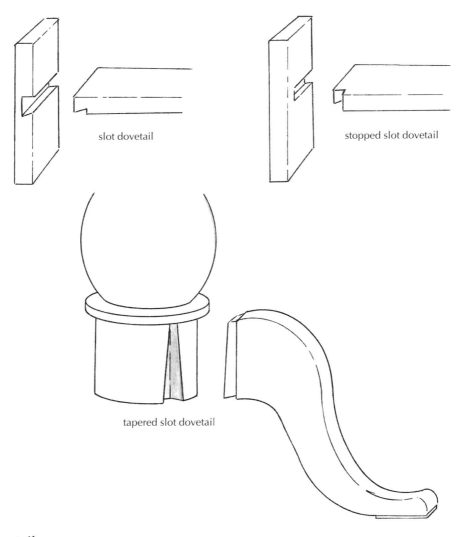

slot dovetail

stopped slot dovetail

tapered slot dovetail

Slot dovetails.

initially and then to slowly pare away the sloping sides.

MITRE JOINTS

The plain mitre joint is used in many situations where two pieces of wood have to be joined at the edge without the end grain showing; plinths, cornices and mouldings in general are joined in this way. In many cases where, for instance, the moulding is supported on the carcase of a cabinet, glue alone or possibly a small pin will be enough to hold the mitre together. In other circumstances where the item needs to support some weight (as in a plinth) or where the moulding is unsupported (as in a picture frame) additional fixings will be required.

SKEW NAILING

With rough work and painted skirting boards, for instance, skew or dovetail nailing will be enough to hold the mitre.

Mitre joints.

REBATED MITRED BUTT JOINT

In setting this joint out, both pieces are rebated as shown below and the projecting part mitred. It is possible to give this joint additional strength by dowelling if it is felt necessary and if the thickness of the timber permits.

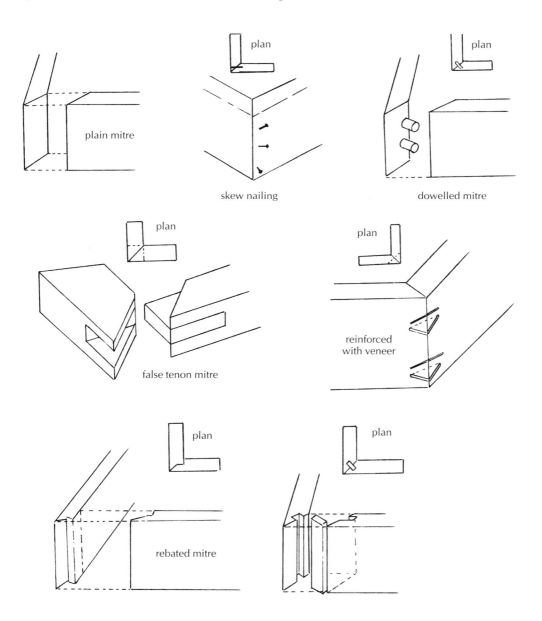

plan

plain mitre

plan

skew nailing

plan

dowelled mitre

plan

false tenon mitre

plan

reinforced with veneer

plan

rebated mitre

plan

DOWELLED MITRE

The ordinary mitre can be greatly strengthened by dowelling, but the dowel must be accurately placed and not too near to the outside edge. The difficulty is in cramping the mitre together while the glue dries. This may be done either by gluing angled blocks on to the sides which are removed and cleaned up later, or by having longer pieces of wood which can have the blocks securely fixed to them, cramped to the sides.

FALSE TENON MITRE

Another method of strengthening a mitre joint is to include a false tenon. Both halves of the mitre are grooved to take a hardwood tongue, as shown. The tongue is cut with cross grain and the groove must not be too close to the outside edge.

REINFORCING WITH VENEER

A mitre can be reinforced by cutting angled slots across the joint and inserting hardwood veneers. It is easier to cut and insert the veneers after the mitre has been glued.

One relatively quick way of assembling a mitred frame is as follows. Lay the four sides of the frame out in a line against a straight edge and with the outer sides uppermost. Stretch masking tape across the joins, insert glue in the mitres and assemble the frame. The last joint will have to be secured with masking tape.

DOWELLING

Dowelling is an increasingly popular way of making a joint because it is both strong and quick to execute. The dowels themselves come in a variety of diameters and may be purchased as long lengths to be cut to size, or ready cut to length with grooving down the side and the ends chamfered.

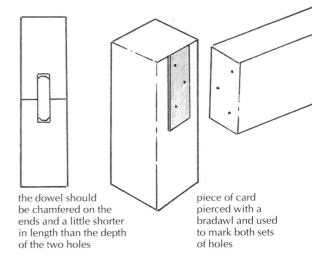

the dowel should be chamfered on the ends and a little shorter in length than the depth of the two holes

piece of card pierced with a bradawl and used to mark both sets of holes

Dowel joints.

The purpose of the grooving is to allow any excess of glue and the air to escape easily from the joint. The grooving is not always necessary; some workers just plane a small flat on one side of the dowel or leave it plain, but the chamfer is always needed.

When deciding on the size of dowel to use, a handy rule of thumb is to use a dowel that is one-third in diameter of the thickness of the timber being dowelled, and at least one-and-a-half times the thickness of the timber in length for each half of the hole. This is not a hard and fast rule and there will be occasions, as with the headrail of a chair, when a longer dowel is desirable because of the short grain. Remember that in all circumstances the dowel should be a little shorter than the combined depths of the two holes, in order to accommodate a small excess of glue.

The main problem with dowelling is in getting the dowel holes to line up, and the best way to accomplish this is to either use a dowel jig or make a template. There are a few dowelling jigs on the market, but these usually deal with only two or three dowels at a time and will not suit all circumstances. One template has all ready been described earlier in this chapter in the section on edge joints, but another type can be made from a piece of stiff card as shown. Cut the card to the exact size of the wood and accurately mark the positions of the dowels on it; the card can then be carefully pierced with a bradawl and used to mark both sets of holes.

It is just as important to drill all dowel holes in line with each other as it is to ensure that they are in the right place. When two pieces of wood are to be joined with a dowel it is no good the dowel's emerging from one piece perfectly straight if the hole in the other piece is at an angle. Use a square to help in keeping the bit in line while drilling.

KNUCKLE OR HINGE JOINT

The hinge joint is used for the supporting brace on small drop-leaf tables such as the Pembroke or Sutherland types. The joint is

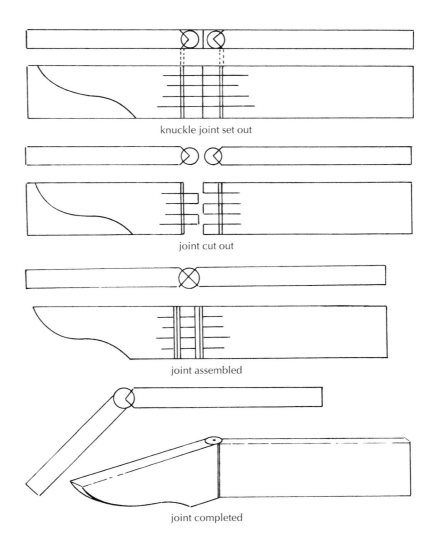

knuckle joint set out

joint cut out

joint assembled

Knuckle or hinge joint.

joint completed

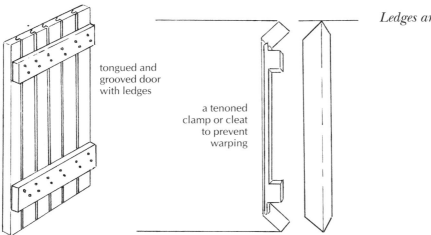

tongued and grooved door with ledges

a tenoned clamp or cleat to prevent warping

Ledges and cleats.

set out by first scribing a centre line on both edges at the ends to be joined; a circle is then drawn at the end, having a diameter equal to the thickness of the wood. Lines are then drawn from the centre of the circle towards the edges at 45 degrees and pointing away from the end. From the point where this line crosses the circumference of the circle a line is squared to the edge of the wood and down both sides. A hole is now drilled, linking the centres of the circles. It is best to drill the holes from each end, starting with a small one and finishing with one that will just accept the shank of a 6in wire nail. The sides are then equally divided into five or seven sections, depending on the size of the timber, five being by far the more usual number. The waste is then cut out, back to the line on the side, so that the two castellated ends fit one into the other. The ends of the timber are now rounded to the circumference of the circle and enough waste is removed beyond the line to allow the centre holes to line up. Waste from the side may now be removed down to the circumference and up to the 45-degrees shoulder line; the shank of the 6in nail is inserted to act as a pivot and the joint can be finely cleaned up with the joint in various positions. This is a difficult joint to make and a good exercise for anyone wanting to hone his woodworking skills.

LEDGES

Whereas cramps are used to hold boards together while glue is setting and are then removed, ledges are pieces of wood nailed to or screwed across the boards and left in position. Ledges are commonly seen on tongued and grooved doors and on the underside of tabletops. It is a good idea to allow for shrinkage when fitting a ledge by screwing it in place rather than nailing it and also using countersunk slots for all but the centre screw.

CLEAT OR CLAMP

A cleat is a piece of wood with the grain lengthways which is secured to the ends of boards to prevent their warping. It may be joined by means of tongue and groove, rebate, dowel or haunched mortise and tenon as shown above.

RULER JOINT

The ruler joint is used to give support along the whole length of a table's drop leaf. It is used in conjunction with a ruler joint hinge. *See* Chapter 13 for fitting hinges.

12

Construction

DOORS

LEDGED AND BRACED DOORS

The ledged and braced door is of simple construction, comprising tongued and grooved match boarding, usually vee-jointed and held together with three ledges, one each at the top, the middle and the bottom of the door. The top surfaces of the ledges should be chamfered to prevent a build up of moisture. Between the ledges are two diagonal braces which help to prevent the door from sagging. The braces are angled across the door so that the top of the brace is on the closing side of it away from the hinges and the bottom of the brace on the hinge side. Both the ledges and the braces are nailed to the match boarding, and the braces are nor-mally let in slightly to the ledges as shown. The match boarding is usually 100 × 15mm and the ledges and braces are nor-mally made from 32mm thick timber.

The positioning of the braces means that the doors are 'handed', that is to say, that the hinges can only be fitted on one side and when purchasing them you will have to state whether you require a left- or a right-hand door. To determine the hand of a door imagine that you are looking at it from the inside, so that the hinges are on view. If the hinges are on the left it is left-handed; if they are on the right it is right-handed. No glue is used in the con-struction of a ledged and braced door, but a good quality wood primer should be used on all parts before it is assembled. Ledged and braced doors that are often used as a gate in close-boarded fences are

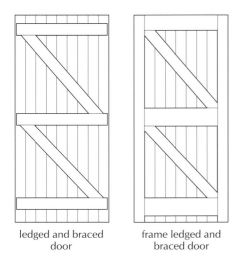

ledged and braced door

frame ledged and braced door

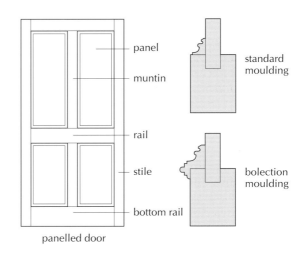

panel

muntin

rail

stile

bottom rail

standard moulding

bolection moulding

panelled door

Different types of door.

normally hung with tee-hinges and fitted with a Suffolk latch and security bolts.

FRAMED LEDGED AND BRACED DOORS

This is essentially the same as the ledged and braced door but has the addition of two stiles and a top rail. The top rail is jointed into the side stiles with a haunched mortise and tenon and the middle and the bottom ledges are jointed to the stiles with barefaced tenons. The match boarding is tongued and grooved into the side stiles and the underside of the top rail. The mortise and tenon joints should be glued with exterior wood glue and the other components primed as with the ledged and braced door. Because of the side stiles, these doors are normally hung with butt hinges. They may also be fitted with a Suffolk latch, but a rim lock is more usual as these doors are often used on sheds and outbuildings.

PANELLED DOORS

Panelled doors are used in both interior and exterior situations, the exterior door being made of thicker material. The doors are constructed with two upright stiles, the one on the hinge side being the hinge stile and the other the closing stile. The members that cross the door horizontally are the rails. All doors will have a top and a bottom stile, the bottom one usually being wider than the top. There is normally at least one other 'middle' rail, but there could be any number of rails depending on how many panels the door has. If there is only the one middle rail, this is usually wider than the stiles. If the width of the door is divided, this is done with vertical members called 'muntins'. The muntins are always jointed between the rails with stub tenons. The panels may be made from a variety of materials depending on the

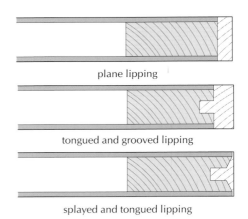

plane lipping

tongued and grooved lipping

splayed and tongued lipping

Flush door lippings.

position and the quality of the door. An exterior door may well have a hardwood panel, but an interior one is more likely to be of plywood. Cheaper doors will probable have an ordinary flat panel, but better quality doors may well have fielded panels.

The panels may be fixed in one of several ways. They may be grooved into the stiles and rails, in which case they will have to be fitted at the same time as the door is assembled. They may be secured into rebates with a bead, the bead being mitred at the corners and pinned in place around the panel, or they may be beaded on both sides. A bolection moulding is one that is designed to fit over the rebate formed between the face of the panel and the side of the stile. The moulding is secured with a small screw from the opposite side of the panel and the head of the screw is covered with a small, moulded bead.

Glass panels in either full- or half-glazed doors are secured into rebates with beads, but more often with putty so that they are easy to change if the glass should be broken.

FLUSH DOORS

These interior doors are called flush doors because both sides are covered with a flush

Door frames and linings.

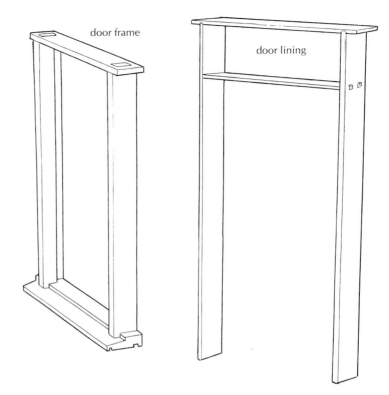

door frame

door lining

panel, usually of plywood. The edges of the door are finished with an edging strip or lipping which may be one of three types: plain lipping, which is just a thin strip of wood 6–10mm (0.2–0.4in) thick and glued in place; tongued and grooved lipping, which is of similar size but tongued and grooved into the door's softwood stile; and splayed and tongued lipping, which has the shoulders of the lipping chamfered so that they do not show on the face of the door.

The interior of the cheaper door is simply a softwood frame filled with corrugated or honeycomb cardboard; the better quality door will have some softwood cross rails as well as uprights. The framework is of the simplest kind with the rails being butt-jointed to the stiles with possibly the addition of a dowel or corrugated 'dog'. Both types of door should be fitted with a piece of solid timber where the lock will be positioned.

DOOR FRAMES AND LININGS

DOOR FRAMES

Door frames are much more solid structures than door linings and are used mostly for exterior doors. The vertical side members or jambs are tenoned into the head and the sill, where used. The door stop is often rebated into the jamb rather than being a separate piece moulding which is nailed on, as is the case with door linings. The sill will normally be made of hardwood to give better wear, even when the rest of the frame is softwood.

DOOR LININGS

Door linings are constructed from lighter material than door frames, have plantedon doorstops and are used exclusively on interior doors. The linings seldom have sills and the jambs are usually housed into the head which protrudes beyond them. Some linings incorporate a window above the door to allow more light to a part of a building where there is no or only inadequate, natural light. The rail between the top of the door and the bottom of the window is called the transom and the frame itself is called a 'borrowed light frame' or, if it extends from floor to ceiling, a 'storey frame'. As a general rule, frames are built in as the building progresses, being propped in place until the brickwork is completed; linings, on the other hand, are not usually fitted until after the brick or blockwork has been finished. Usually the opening left in internal brick or blockwork is slightly wider than the size of the door lining in order to allow for packing wedges to be inserted between the lining and the brickwork. This is done so that final adjustment may be made to straighten the lining which, because, of its light construction, may have some distortion that would make the fitting of the door more difficult.

WINDOWS

CASEMENT WINDOWS

The casement window consists of an outer frame made up of two side jambs, a head rail and a sill. The height of the window may be divided by a transom rail and the width by a mullion. Any mullion will normally project above the transom rail. All the joints used in the construction of the window frame are conventional mortise and tenon. The inner, opening frames are called casements and are of a lighter construction. Any glazed section of the window which does not open is known as a fixed sash. The side uprights of the casement are the stiles and the members joining these at the top and the bottom of the frame are the top and bottom rails. The rails are tenoned into the stiles, but, because of the light construction, a conventional haunched tenon would cut away too much of the rail and thus a franked mortise and tenon is sometimes used. Instead of the haunch being left on the tenon it is left on the mortised stile and the rail is cut away to receive it.

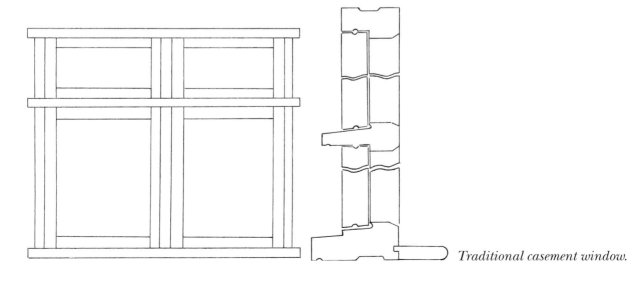

Traditional casement window.

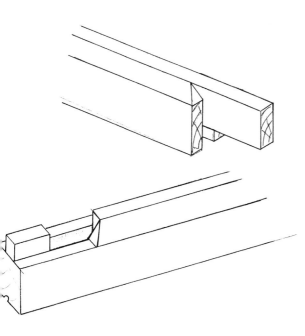

Franked mortise and tenon.

STORM-PROOF WINDOWS

The difference between storm-proof and ordinary casement windows is that the former have the sash rebated into the frame. This means that the joint is covered and that there is less likelihood of driving rain getting in past the joint.

Casement Furniture
The ordinary casement sash is hung with standard butt hinges but the storm-proof window has a special cranked hinge to compensate for the rebate. Casement windows are fitted with a stay which consists of a pivoted arm with a series of holes in it that locate on a pin fixed to the window frame. This allows the window to be opened to a varying extent without the danger of its blowing closed. The fastener is fitted to the sash stile and locates into a mortise in the frame which is covered with a slotted metal plate.

SLIDING SASH WINDOW

This type of window is little used now but was at one time the most common window to be seen. It is for this reason that it is still widely found and it is included here because many listed buildings may have only this type of window fitted.

The sashes themselves, an inner and an outer, slide up and down for opening in a box-section frame and are counterbalanced with cast-iron weights attached to the sash with a stout cord threaded through a pulley.

The box sections of the side frame are made up of an outer and an inner lining which are joined together at the back with a back lining of thin wood or plywood and with a more substantial pulley stile at the front. A parting bead is grooved into the pulley stile to separate the top and the

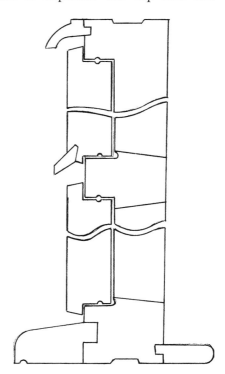

Storm-proof casement.

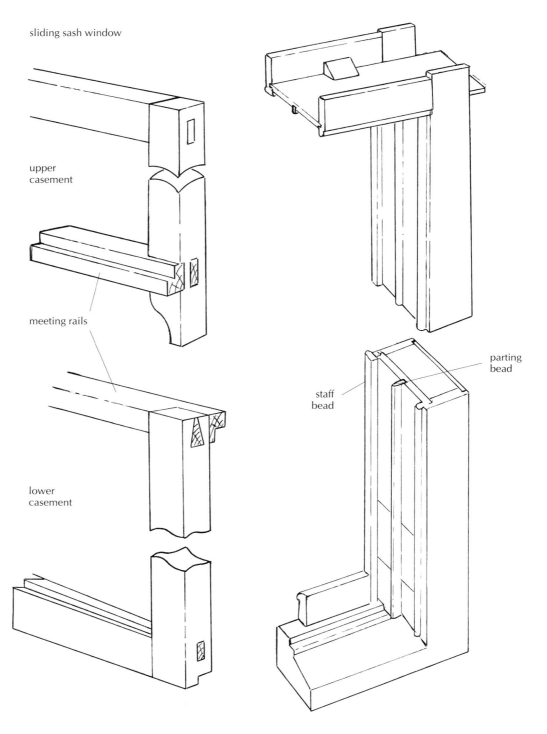

sliding sash window

upper
casement

meeting rails

lower
casement

staff
bead

parting
bead

The sash window.

bottom sash and a 'staff' bead is applied to the inside of the frame to keep the sashes in place. The sill is made from solid timber, but the top rail is another box section. The pulley wheels are let into the top of the pulley stiles and a pocket is cut in the bottom of the pulley stile to allow the weights to be removed when the sash cords need to be replaced.

The sash rails are tenoned into the sash stiles with franked mortise and tenon joints. The top rail of the lower sash and the bottom rail of the upper sash meet when the window is fully closed and are known as the meeting rails. The meeting rails are wider to make up the gap between the two sashes and the faces of the rails are shaped to fit together closely to keep out the weather. The ends of these two rails will have to be cut away slightly to make room for the parting bead, and it is on the top of these rails that the catch is fitted which locks the window. The stiles of the upper sash are extended down past the bottom rail so that a through mortise can be used and this extension is known as a joggle. This cannot be done to the upper rail of the bottom sash and it is usual to make the tenon dovetail shaped so that it will not pull away when the rail is used to open the window.

To fit the sash cords a 'mouse' is required. This a weight, sometimes of lead but often a piece of chain, attached to a length of twine that can be threaded though the pulley. One end of the twine is attached to the end of the sash cord and the weighted end of the mouse is threaded through the pulley so that it drops down on the inside of the box section to the sash pocket, pulling the cord with it. This end of the cord is then untied from the twine and fixed to the sash weight. The cord is then cut to the length required and a large knot tied in the end to prevent its pulling all the way through the pulley. The process is repeated for the other

three cords and then the cords may be secured to the sashes.

The outside of the sash stile has a groove down it sometimes ending in a small, round recess to house the cord. This is secured in the groove with a galvanized clout nail. The upper sash is corded first, and then the parting bead is inserted before the lower sash is corded. Once the two sashes are in place and the operation has been checked, the staff bead is nailed in place and the catch can be fitted. Sash bolts may be fitted for extra security to bolt the two sashes together to prevent their being opened.

FLOORS

GROUND FLOOR

The floor joists on which the actual floor rests are usually 100×50mm sawn softwood and rest on a 100×50mm sawn softwood wallplate. The wallplate is bedded above the damp-proof course on to a sleeper wall with sand and cement. The sleeper wall is built near to but not touching the external wall and, when the joists are laid on top of the wallplate, they are nailed in place; it must be ensured that the ends of the joists do not touch the external wall. Further sleeper walls are built with their centres about 1.8m (71in) apart. If a fireplace is to be installed a concrete hearth must be built at least 125mm (5in) thick and extending beyond the breast by at least 500mm (20in) at the front and 150mm (6in) at the sides. No timber must come nearer to the fireplace than these measurements, however, because the Building Regulations change from time to time and from area to area it is always necessary to check them with your local authority before starting any project of this type.

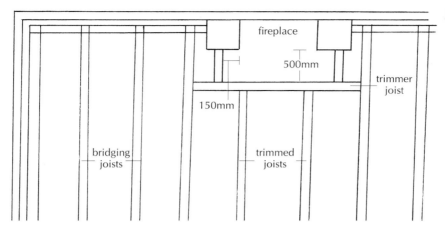

Floor joists.

fireplace

500mm

150mm

trimmer joist

bridging joists

trimmed joists

UPPER FLOORS

When constructing floors above ground-floor level it is not possible to include sleeper walls, so the joists will have to span from wall to wall. These joists are known as bridging joists and they have to be much wider in depth than those for the ground floor. The size of the joist will be determined at the design stage, but a rough rule of thumb is to divide the span in decimetres by two and add two – this will give the size in centimetres. That is to say, that if the span of a room is 4m or 40dm, the calculation will be done as follows: 40 divided by 2 equals 20, add 2 and this equals 22. The depth of the joists will therefore be 22cm. As this is not a standard size the practical thing to do is to go up to the nearest standard size; in this case that will be 22.5cm. There are several ways in which the joists can be supported:

Direct Bearing
The inner wall is built up to the level of the underside of the joist and the joist is rested on it direct.

Built-In Wallplate
This is similar to the direct-bearing method except that a wallplate is bedded in on top of the inner wall.

Corbel and Wallplate
In this method wrought-iron brackets or corbels are built into the brickwork and a wallplate is rested on them. This is not used in domestic situations because the bracket and wallplate are visible from the floor below.

Joist Hangers
These are steel brackets or shoes which hang and are screwed on to the wall; they are easy to use and are approved by all authorities.

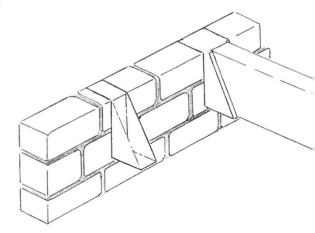

Joist hangers.

Trimmed Joists

Sometimes bridging joists do not span the whole width of a room but end at a trimmer joist, that is, one which lines an opening in the floor such as a stairwell. The joist which is tenoned into a trimming joist is called a trimmer joist. Where joist hangers are not used the trimming is achieved with a tusk tenon.

Strutting

Over a long span there is always a chance that the joist will twist and distort the floor. To counteract this struts are placed in rows at intervals of about 3.5m (138in). The struts themselves may be off-cuts of joist cut to fit between the bridging joists or they may be herringbone strutting. The latter consists of pairs of battens cut and fitted diagonally between the joists. The battens are nailed to the joists at each end, having had a saw cut made there to prevent splitting.

FLOORING

THE SQUARE-EDGE BOARD

Common floorboards with square edges are not used much now as they tend to shrink and warp too much for a satisfactory surface. However, when used, they are nailed across the floor joists with floor brads, any joints being made direct over a joist. The boards are cramped up tightly together for nailing with either a special floorboard cramp which is designed to fit over a joist or with folding wedges. Folding wedges are simply a pair of wedges cut from the board being laid. One part is temporarily nailed to the joist a little way from the last board and the other is then hammered in between them to force the boards together for nailing. When a joint has to be made in the length of the board, it is made

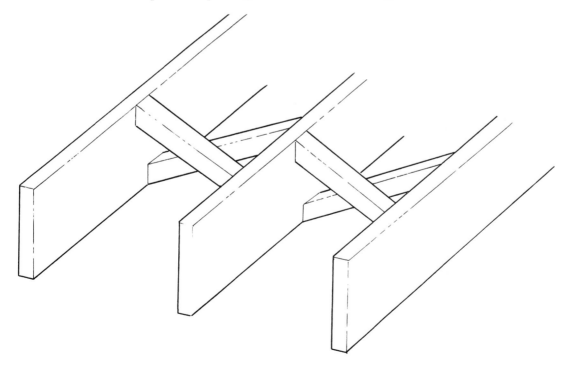

Strutting.

in one of two ways, but always over a joist: either the end of each board can be cut square, with each board taking up half the width of the joist, or the first board can overlap the joist by up to two-thirds and be cut at an angle. The second board is then cut at the corresponding angle and laid on top. This joint has the advantage of having to be nailed only once but it takes longer to make. Nails must be used only at the sides of the boards, never in the centre where wires or pipes could be located.

TONGUED AND GROOVED BOARD

Tongued and grooved boards are laid in the same way as square-edge boards, with the folding wedges being cut from tongued and grooved board to protect the edges. Tongued and grooved boards come in two types: one with a conventional tongue and groove and one with a long tapering shoulder which allows it to be secretly nailed. The standard T and G floorboards have the tongue slightly off-centre and are laid

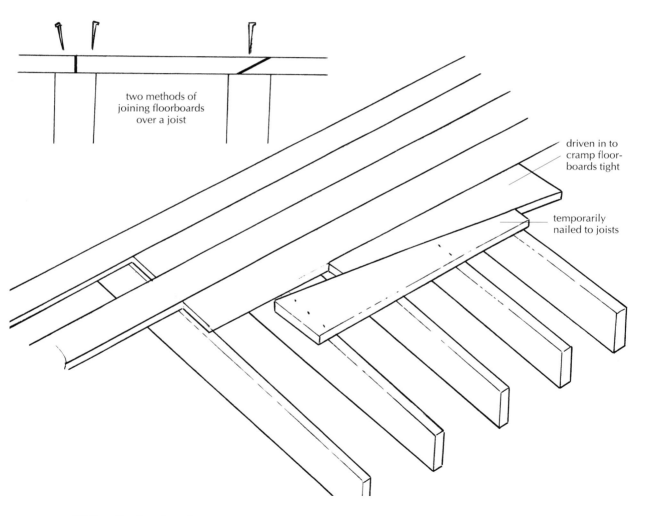

two methods of
joining floorboards
over a joist

driven in to
cramp floor-
boards tight

temporarily
nailed to joists

Fitting the floorboards.

with the larger shoulder uppermost to allow for wear in use.

CHIPBOARD FLOORING

Chipboard flooring has the advantage of allowing a large area of floor to be covered quickly, but holes have to be cut for access to services at convenient points before the floor is fixed because of the difficulty of locating them afterwards.

PARTITION WALLS

A partition wall is essentially a softwood framework of 50mm-thick sawn timber which is either 75 or 100mm wide, depending on the requirements, and covered with a sheet material of some kind, usually plasterboard. Walls of this type are non-load bearing and may have door-opening or glazed-window sections if needed. They are constructed with a horizontal head and floor plate together with vertical wall plates. Intermediate vertical timbers or 'studs' are placed at intervals to match the size of the facing sheet material and horizontal 'noggings' are nailed between the studs to prevent distortion and to provide convenient jointing positions for the covering sheet material.

It is important that the wall, head and floor plates are well secured to ensure that the structure is rigid when completed. It is normal to fix the wall and floor plates with rawlplugs, but the ceiling or head plate may be more of a problem. Where the partition wall is running at right angles to the ceiling joists these can be located and the head plate fastened to them where they cross. If the partition wall is running parallel to the ceiling joists and is not located directly under one, then bridging pieces or noggings will have to

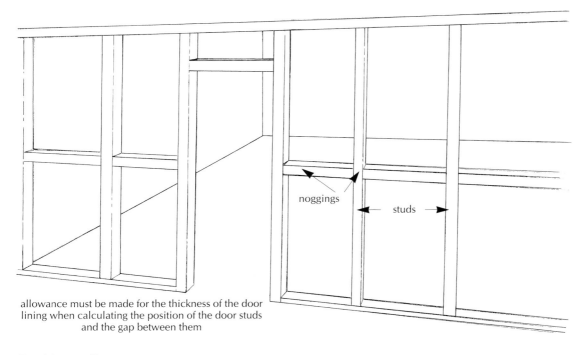

noggings

studs

allowance must be made for the thickness of the door lining when calculating the position of the door studs and the gap between them

Partition wall.

be placed between the joists to provide a securing point for the head or ceiling plate.

DOOR OPENING

Where a door opening is to be included in the partition it is best if the door stud is jointed to the floor plate rather than simply nailed; it is also better if the head nogging is jointed. Allowance must be made for the thickness of the door lining when calculating the position of the door studs and the gap between them. It is recommended that, in addition to the thickness of the lining timber, a further 25mm (1in) should be allowed for on each side. This is so that there will be a gap of that amount between the back of the lining and the stud. This will allow for folding wedges and packing to be inserted in that gap in order to ensure that the lining is absolutely straight and square. The width of the lining will have to be that of the studs plus whatever facing material is being used. The

joint between the lining and the facing material is covered with an architrave.

STAIRS

Staircases come in so many different forms that it would be possible to write a book on this aspect of woodwork alone and still find more aspects to cover. For that reason we shall look only at the basic single flight.

The first two things that we need to know when planning a staircase are the total 'going' and the total 'rise' and so it may be as well to be familiar with the terms associated with staircases before we start.

Flight: the total number of steps in any straight line.

Going: the horizontal distance between the front of one tread and the next.

Newel post: the posts at the top and the bottom of a flight into which the strings are tenoned.

Rise: the vertical distance between the top of one tread and the next.

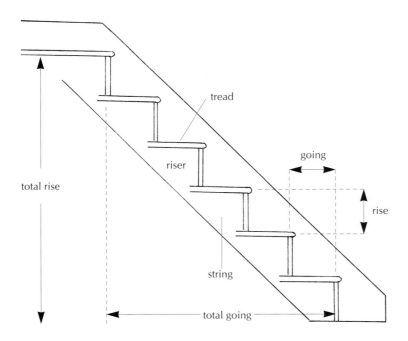

Terms associated with a staircase.

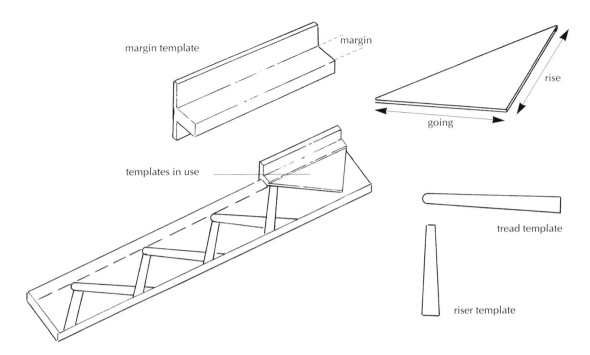

Marking out the string.

Riser: the vertical board between and at the back of two treads.

Step: one tread and one riser together.

String: the sloping side boards of the stairs into which the other components fix; if the stairs are against a wall, the string fixed to the wall is the wall string and the other side is the outer string.

Total going: the horizontal distance between the front of the first and the last tread.

Total rise: the vertical distance between the finished floor line at the bottom and the finished floor line at the top.

Tread: the horizontal board that is stepped on when using the stairs.

Once the total rise and the total going have been measured – and it must be remembered that there will be Building Regulations covering this – then the total rise must be divided into equal risers.

The Regulations must be checked before a project of this kind is undertaken, but at present (1999) the pitch of a staircase must not exceed 42 degrees, the going must not exceed 220mm (8.7in) and the rise must not exceed 220mm. In any flight the sum of the going plus twice the rise must be between 550 and 700mm (21.7 and 27.6in). If, for instance, the total rise is 3,225mm (127in), this must be divided by 220 (the maximum rise allowed), giving 14.65. In this case it is clear that fifteen risers will be necessary. Therefore 3,225mm must be divided by 15 giving a rise of 215mm (8.5in).

The number of treads is always one less than the number of risers, so that we require fifteen risers and fourteen treads. If we have a total going of 3,680mm (144.9in) this must be divided by the number of treads, giving us 262.85mm (10.35in). Now if we take the going of

262.85 and add twice the riser, which is 430, we get 692.85, which is just within the maximum of 700.

The next step is to cut the strings from 32mm board which is wide enough to take the treads and risers. Once this has been done, a pitch board and a margin template are made. The pitch board is a triangular piece of plywood with the sides forming the right angle of the exact size of the going and the rise. The margin is the parallel distance from the top edge of the string to the front end of each step, and a baton of this size with a plywood stock attached to form a T will act as a template.

With the pitch board held against the margin template, the floor line may be drawn at one end of the string, followed by the subsequent risers and treads. Both strings must be marked out in this way; you should remember that they are a pair and that one will be the mirror image of the other. Remember also that the outer string will need to have tenons cut at the ends to fit into the newel posts at the top and the bottom of the flight.

Two more templates now need to be made: a riser template and a tread template.

These are cut from plywood and are tapered, one end being the thickness of the tread or riser but the other end being thicker to allow for the fixing wedges. By the use of these templates against the lines already drawn on the strings the marking out is completed.

The rebating is usually done to a depth of 12mm (½ in) and can be done by hand or with an electric router.

Now the treads and the risers are themselves cut to size, and it is normal to have a 25mm (1in) tread with a 12mm (½in) plywood riser which is housed into the underside of it. The amount that the riser is set back from the front edge of the tread is called the 'nosing' and is often the same as the thickness of the riser. The treads and risers are assembled on a 'cradle' which keeps them at right angles while the glue blocks are fixed in place underneath. The assembled 'steps' are then carefully stacked on one side until the glue is dry.

Once the work is complete on the strings and steps the wedges are cut ready for final assembly.

The assembly is best carried out on a sturdy bench where it is possible to keep

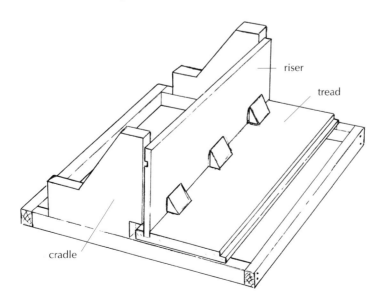

Treads and risers are assembled on a cradle.

Final assembly.

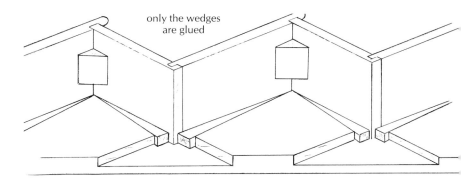

only the wedges
are glued

the strings straight and parallel. It is advisable to fit the wedges methodically, starting with the bottom riser, then the tread and so on up the flight. Remember that it is the wedges only that are glued and once this has been done the risers are screwed to the backs of the treads to prevent movement when in use.

The handrail and the balustrade can now be fitted to the newel posts on the outer string and the stairs are ready to be fitted on site.

ARCHITRAVE AND SKIRTING BOARD

Few things look worse than badly fitting architrave and skirting board mitres; these bad joints seem to show even when they have been filled and painted over. These days more and more people prefer to see a natural wood finish to the woodwork in a room rather than a painted one, and this makes good joints even more important.

The tools required are a well-sharpened tenon saw and a good mitre block. I recommend the combined adjustable mitre table and saws that are widely available at builders' merchants and DIY stores. These saws may be set to a variety of preset angles and they cut very accurately. Of course, if you can afford to buy a powered mitre saw

or a radial arm saw the speed and accuracy of cut is even greater.

ARCHITRAVE

In theory, one should be able to measure the lengths of the side and the top architrave, cut mitres on the top of the side pieces, mitre each end of the top piece, and the whole will fit in place around the door or window perfectly. In practice this would be a miracle, each length will require marking in place.

First decide how far away from the edge of the frame the architrave is to fit and mark these points at the top of the frame. Hold a length of architrave in place across the top of the door frame or window and transfer these marks on to the bottom, thin edge of the architrave. Transfer the architrave to the mitre saw and cut the mitres at each end. The outside or thick edge of the architrave should be the longer one and the pencil marks that were made on the thin, inner edge should be just left in by the saw cut. This top length should now be nailed in place; but at this stage the nails must be left proud so that they may be easily removed if necessary. The nails should be placed in the recesses of the moulding so that they will be less visible when driven home. Take another length of architrave and, making sure that the bottom end is square, stand it in place on one side of the

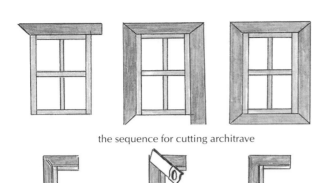

the sequence for cutting architrave

the joint can be adjusted slightly with a saw cut

Architrave.

door. Holding the new length in place against the top mitre, mark the inner, thin edge where it meets the top architrave. Transfer this length to the mitre saw and cut the mitre. It is good practice to cut the length over size by about 1mm to ensure a tight fit. Hold this second length in place and check the accuracy of the joint. If the joint is open at the front but touches at the back, a little of the wood from the back may be pared away with a sharp chisel, taking care not to touch the front of the moulding. If the angle does not quite fit, then temporarily nail the architrave in place with the joint as close as possible. Now, with a tenon saw cut along the joint line. This will remove a small amount of wood from each side where the joint touches, and the joint should then be perfect. Repeat these procedures for the other side of the door and nail the architrave in place, driving the nails home with a nail punch. A locking nail is then driven into the joint itself from the top to prevent the joint from opening up as the wood shrinks. This locking nail must be placed where the moulding is thickest to minimize the risk of splitting or of the nail's coming through the moulding.

SKIRTING BOARD

There are two types of mitre which may be encountered with skirting boards; these are the internal and the external mitre. If you imagine an alcove in a room, the skirting that goes along the back wall will meet the wall forming the chimney breast with an internal mitre. That is to say, that the back of the skirting board will be longer than the front. However, where the board along the side of the chimney breast meets the front wall there will be an external mitre, as the back of the board will be shorter than the front.

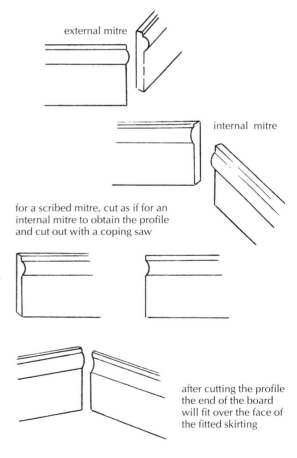

external mitre

internal mitre

for a scribed mitre, cut as if for an internal mitre to obtain the profile and cut out with a coping saw

after cutting the profile the end of the board will fit over the face of the fitted skirting

Skirting mitres.

External Mitres

If the two walls meet at right angles then the two ends of skirting can be mitred at 45 degrees and lock-nailed each way after fitting. If the walls are meant to meet at right angles but are slightly out, the joint can be adjusted in one of the following ways. If the joint is open at the front then a little wood may be pared away from the back with a chisel, taking care not to touch the front edge. It the joint is open at the back, a little wood should be taken with a plane. It will be necessary to adjust both pieces somewhat unless the gap is very small. If the walls do not meet at right angles then the angle will have to be bisected so that the same angle is cut on each piece of skirting. It is no good cutting one length to 45 degrees and thinking that the other one can be adjusted. Unless both pieces are cut to the same angle one face will be larger than the other and stick out proud. To set a bevel to the correct angle a piece of card is held flat on the floor across the face of the joint and the line of each wall drawn on it. This is done by placing a straight edge against the face of the wall and extending out over the card. When the angle has been drawn on the card there are two options, either you can bisect the angle, as explained in Chapter 8, or you can set the bevel by trial and error, testing it against each line until the angles coincide.

Internal Mitres

Internal mitres can be cut in much the same way as external ones or they may be scribed. To make a scribed joint, cut and fix a piece of skirting board so that the end butts tightly into the corner with a square end. Now cut a mitre on the end of the piece of skirting that will fit against it, as if you were cutting a conventional internal mitre. The face of the cut end will be a profile of the board. This profile is carefully cut out with a coping saw, with the result that the end will now fit exactly against the face of the fitted skirting board.

GLASS CUTTING AND FITTING

Glass cutting is something that many people avoid at all costs, and it is true that your local glazier will cut anything you could want. In fact, glass cutting is not too difficult, and in most cases what is lacking is not the ability to cut glass but the confidence to try.

The first requirement is a flat, clean surface on which to work and the second is a good glass cutter. A single wheel cutter is the one most professionals will use, although you can go to the expense of a diamond cutter if you wish. You will need a straight edge to run the cutter against for making straight cuts, one that is not too narrow, to allow you to hold it firmly in place on the glass.

If you are replacing a pane in a window, the frame will have to be well cleaned out before it is possible to measure for the new glass. Always wear a thick pair of gardening gloves when handling broken glass. Remove all the loose pieces first and then the putty surrounding the rest. If the frame is a sturdy one the putty may be removed with the aid of an old chisel and a mallet, but be sure to wear protective clothing and goggles. Take a little at a time where the putty is holding fast, and try to remove it without marking the frame too much. If the frame is delicate, such as with the tracery door on a cabinet, then the putty will have to be softened and removed carefully with the chisel alone. The putty can be softened with the use of a hot soldering iron and, quite often, pushing the soldering iron along the frame will be enough to remove the putty without the need for a chisel. Take care, because somewhere under the putty will be the pins or little triangles of zinc which hold the glass in place; these too will have to be removed. Once the old frame is clean it is possible to take the measurement of the glass. When measuring its

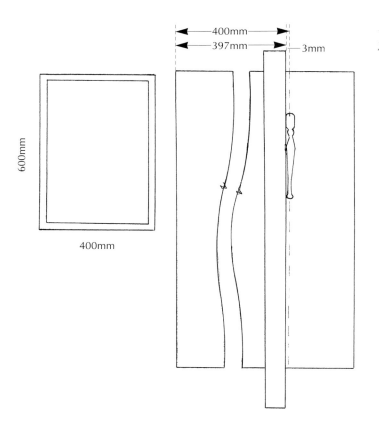

400mm

397mm

3mm

600mm

400mm

*Keep a firm and constant
pressure during the cut.*

size, leave a little tolerance so that the glass is not too tight a fit in the frame.

Lay the sheet of glass to be cut flat on the workbench, preferably over a clean, white dustsheet. Cut the larger dimension first. Measure from one straight side of the glass to the straight edge. Measure both the top and the bottom to ensure that the straight edge is parallel with the side of the pane of glass, and remember to allow for the distance from the edge of the glass cutter to the actual cutting wheel. If the distance from the edge of the cutter to the centre of the cutting wheel is 3mm (0.12in) and the size of glass you require is 400mm (15.75in), then the straight edge should be 397mm (15.63in) from the edge of the glass for cutting. Remember that the finished size of the glass should be a little less than the internal measurement of the frame.

The cutter and the area of glass to be cut should be lubricated with turpentine or methylated spirits before cutting. Starting at the very top of the glass, and keeping the cutter upright and against the straight edge, pull the cutter across the glass in one firm stroke, all the way across until it comes off the opposite edge. Keep a firm and consistent pressure throughout the cut without pressing too hard. Practice will tell you how much pressure is required; it should be firm enough to cut the glass but not so hard that tiny flakes of it appear on the surface.

If it is a relatively small piece of glass that is being cut, it may be brought to the edge of the workbench and positioned so that the cut is directly over the edge of the bench, with the waste glass overhanging. Holding the glass firmly down on the bench, grip the edge of the waste with a

Hold the glass firmly with a gloved hand.

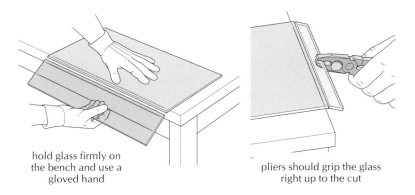

hold glass firmly on
the bench and use a
gloved hand

pliers should grip the glass
right up to the cut

gloved hand and snap down firmly. The cut should break away cleanly, but any little bits of waste which remain may be snipped off by gripping them with the ends of a pair of pliers and snapping downwards. The pliers should grip the waste glass right up to the cut or there is the risk that only some of the waste will be removed.

If, when you have finished the cut with the glass cutter, you do not feel confident of breaking the waste away cleanly in one go – perhaps because it is a long cut – there is an alternative method. Once again bring the cut to the edge of the workbench, with the waste overhanging, but this time position it so that the cut is a few inches away from the bench. Lightly tap with the end of the cutter or the pene of a small hammer on the underside of the cut while supporting the waste glass. Gentle taps along the full length of the cut are all that is required and the glass should come away in your hand. Another way of dealing with larger sheets of glass is to slip the straight edge underneath the cut. Place another piece of wood of the same thickness as the straight edge also under the glass, so that the piece required is supported, and apply downward pressure to the waste or off-cut. On a long cut the downward force is best applied with a batten so that the pressure is distributed along the length of the cut; this will reduce the possibility that only some of the off-cut will break away. The reason for

wanting the off-cuts to break away in one piece is that any split between sections of off-cut could continue past the cut line, into the piece of glass we want. Check the glass for size after cutting and if all is well the other edges may be cut in the same way.

CUTTING CURVES

Unlike straight cuts that can be measured from one edge and cut against a straight edge, curved cuts have to be marked out in some way so that they can be followed with the cutter. There are several ways of doing this and you will have to decide which one is the best for any job you undertake. First, it is best to make a cardboard template of the exact size of the required glass. This can usually be done by holding the cardboard over the frame and marking the inside edge with a pencil. Cut the template out just inside the pencil line, and remember that you need to make it a little smaller than the inside of the frame so that it is not too tight a fit. On most windows there is plenty of tolerance, but with some glazed cabinets this may be quite small. Place the template in the frame to check, and adjust it with a pair of scissors if necessary. Now you have a choice to make: you may place the template on the glass and draw round it with an appropriate marker pen, or you may place the template underneath the glass and follow its outline with the cutter

113

through the glass. If you choose the latter, you will have to make sure that you view from directly above the template, otherwise it may look as if the cutter is over the edge of the template when in fact it is not. This is not much of a problem on thin glass but on plate glass, where there is a greater distance between the template and the cutter, it may make a considerable difference. When breaking away the off-cuts from curves it is advisable to tap the cut line from underneath, as explained earlier, until the two parts separate. On very tight curves it is a good idea to hatch-cut the glass so that the waste part breaks away in small pieces. If an internal point is required this can be drilled with a glass-cutting drill at the intersection of the two cuts to prevent their continuing too far.

FITTING THE GLASS

Window Frames

The inside of the frame should be painted with an oil-based paint before the bedding putty is applied and, preferably, the putty should be applied before the paint has fully dried. This will ensure the maximum adhesion of the putty to the wood. My father, who was a professional builder, would never use the word putty on its own. He would never say to me, 'Use putty for this or that'; it was always 'Use paint and putty'. Bearing this in mind, when the glass is bedded in place and secured with pins around edges, the next job is to paint that part of the glass which will be covered with putty. Allow the paint to start drying and then apply the putty, pushing it into place with the thumb all around the edge. The excess of putty is removed with the blade of a putty knife. The knife is pulled along the glazing bar with its point against the glass, leaving a clean face. The putty must then be allowed to dry for some time before it is painted, and, when painting, the cutting in

must be done ensuring that the paint just comes over the edge of the putty on to the glass to form a weatherproof seal. If the putty is very sticky and tends to adhere to the knife, the knife should be dipped in water and this will solve the problem; likewise, putty will tend not to stick to wet hands.

Glazed Cabinets

Most glazed cabinets will have the glass held in with wooden beads; but the shaped glass of tracery doors and the like will be held by putty. The putty may be coloured by mixing in powdered pigments such as brown umber or burnt sienna, which are purchased from polishing suppliers. The powders will make the putty dry and therefore linseed oil will also have to be added. The glass is bedded in on a thin layer of putty and held in place with small veneer pins or glazier's 'sprigs', small triangular pieces of metal. If the glazing bars are too delicate to take the pins or sprigs being hammered in, they may be squeezed into place with pliers.

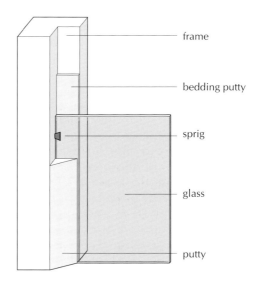

The glass is held in place with glazier's sprigs.

13

Metal Fittings

HINGES

BUTT HINGES

This is most the common hinge for fitting doors of all descriptions and can be purchased in steel or brass. The number of hinges required for any door is determined by its weight and size. Two hinges are usually sufficient for cupboard doors, but three or even four will be required for heavy exterior doors or doors which have heavy glass panels. The positions of the ends of the hinge are marked on the door and a marking gauge is set to the bare thickness of the hinge at the knuckle. A line is then scribed on the face of the door between the end marks. A second marking gauge is set by placing the stock against the edge of the hinge and the point open to the centre of the hinge pin; this line is then marked on the edge of the door, with the gauge stock against the door face. The waste wood is removed and the hinge screwed in place.

Care must be taken not to let the hinge in too deeply, or the doorway will be hinge-bound and not close properly but spring open. The door is now held in place and the hinge positions marked on the door frame. Lines are squared across the frame and the depth of the hinge is marked. This depth may vary from that marked on the door itself, because the door may or may not be set back a little from the frame. It is possible simply to screw the hinge in place on the door frame, but it is best to cut a tapering recess for the back of the hinge, so as to take the weight of the door off the screws. In some cases, mostly with furniture, the hinge is let equally into the door and the door frame so that the hinge is flush with the open door frame. The butt hinge is always let equally into both components in the case of a box, unless there is an overhanging moulding.

RISING BUTTS

Rising butts are fitted when an obstacle such as a carpet lies in the path of the opening door. The hinge is constructed with a spiral joint which lifts the door on opening and tends to close it when left free. The hinge is fitted in the normal way except that the whole of the knuckle is usually fitted proud of the frame.

PIVOT HINGES

Pivot hinges are fitted to the bottom and the top edge of a door and do not show at

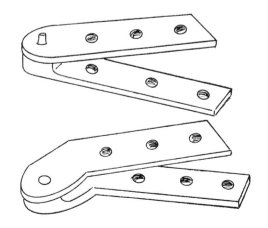

Pivot hinges.

all when the door is closed. They are useful when the door in question is heavy or when the door frame is moulded and a butt hinge

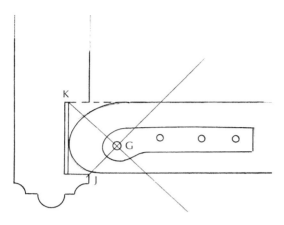

Marking out a pivot hinge.

would spoil the effect. The main point of consideration in fitting this type of hinge is to find the correct position for the centre of the hinge pin. The best way to do this is to make a full-size drawing as shown to the left and to make the ends of the door in the drawing square and, instead of the hollow channel in the door frame, draw this as a rebate ¼in (6mm) deep. From the points J and K draw lines at 45 degrees. Where these two lines meet is the position for the centre of the hinge pin G. Set a compass with the point on G and draw an arc on the edge of the door and another giving ample clearance for the operation of the door. Transfer these marks to the work and set the hinge in flush. Pin or pivot hinges come in both straight and angle-ended forms. Note there is a drop in the lower plate, which prevents the plates from rubbing together.

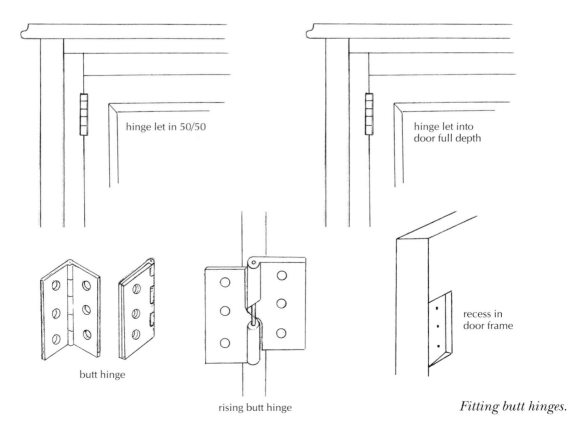

hinge let in 50/50

hinge let into door full depth

butt hinge

rising butt hinge

recess in door frame

Fitting butt hinges.

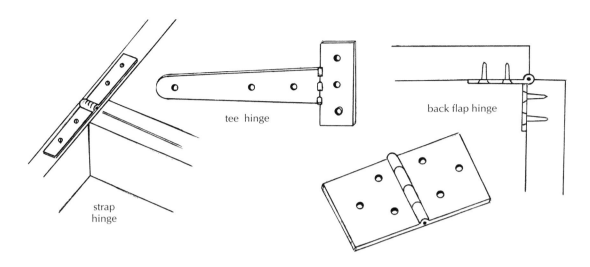

Strap, tee and back flap hinges.

STRAP HINGES

The strap hinge is used in situations where the width of the surface for fixing is limited, as in the case of the writing slope shown above.

TEE HINGES

Tee hinges are mostly to be found on gates, where they give good support to the gate itself, but where room on the post is limited in width.

BACK FLAP HINGES

This hinge is used for drop-leaf tables. The hinge flange is usually square and is countersunk for screws on the opposite side to the butt hinge. When being fitted, the flanges are not sunk into the top or the leaves, because the centre of the pin must be level with the underside of the top and leaves in order to prevent a gap between them when the leaf is in the drop position. When fixing the hinges cut the wood away neatly to receive the knuckles.

RULE JOINT HINGES

This hinge is made for a drop-leaf table which has a rule joint; it is similar to the back flap hinge, except that one flange is longer than the other. The rule joint is employed rather than a butt joint on better quality cabinet work because the hinge is not visible with the flap either up or down. The illustration overleaf shows the setting out of a rule joint. Line *DD* indicates the depth of the hinge flange and line *CC* indicates the shoulder line of the joint. The intersection of *CC* and *DD* is marked *E* and is the centre of the hinge pin. It may be seen that a small gouge will be needed to make a recess for the knuckle. Decide how deep the shoulder is to be and set a compass with its point on *E* to the base of the shoulder and scribe a quarter circle. The waste wood is removed with a rebate or shoulder plane on the top and a moulding plane or gouge on the leaf.

STOP HINGES

The stop hinge is essentially a butt hinge for boxes to prevent the lid from falling all

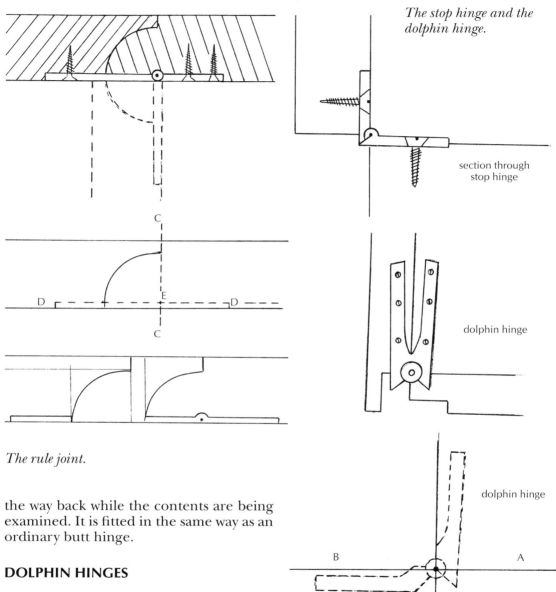

The stop hinge and the dolphin hinge.

section through stop hinge

dolphin hinge

dolphin hinge

The rule joint.

the way back while the contents are being examined. It is fitted in the same way as an ordinary butt hinge.

DOLPHIN HINGES

The dolphin hinge is used for small fall fronts, such as secretaire drawers, which appear to be ordinary drawers but where in reality the front hinges down to form a writing surface. The illustration shows the positioning of the hinge for letting in. The tapered ends stop the hinge from opening too far and keep the writing surface level. When the fall is raised it is held in position with a catch to prevent it from falling when it is pulled out like a drawer. The illustration shows the rebating of the bottom of the drawer front. To mark the position of the hinge, lay the front level with the bottom, in the open position. With the hinge open to its fullest extent, place it against the side, as shown by the dotted lines, taking care that the centre of the pin is where the surfaces of A and B meet, and mark around the hinge with a knife or pencil.

QUADRANT

A quadrant support is used in conjunction with hinges on a secretaire drawer where there is much weight to be supported. In order to fit the quadrant successfully you will have to ascertain the diameter of the circle of which it is part. Place the quadrant on a piece of paper and mark its outline with a fine pencil. Now mark three points A, C and C on the outside line at equal distances apart. Set a compass from A to B and from B scribe the arcs D, E and F, and, with the point on A, scribe arcs G and H. Repeat this procedure from C, scribing arcs J and K. Draw the converging lines and where they meet at U will be the centre of the circle. Make a full-size drawing as shown, and, with K as the centre, scribe the arc L. Place the quadrant against this line and mark the

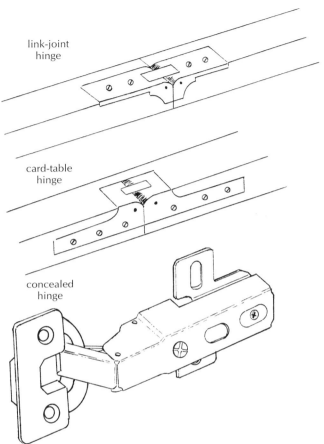

Link-joint, card-table and concealed hinges.

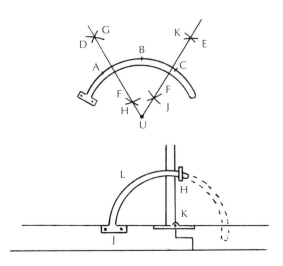

Method of setting out quadrant.

position of the end plate J and the stop plate H. Transfer these marks to the work and set in the quadrant.

LINK-JOINT HINGES

These are made primarily for card tables so that there is no knuckle standing up when the table is open and in use.

CARD-TABLE HINGES

Another kind of hinge designed for card tables, this time fitted to the side rather than the top surface.

THE CONCEALED HINGE

This hinge is now widely used on kitchen and bedroom furniture and comes in a variety of types. They come in two pieces: a plate which is fitted to the carcase and the hinge proper, which is fitted to the door. A special flat drill is required to drill the hole in the door, but once fitted these hinges are easy to align to the cabinet.

LOCKS

MORTISE LOCKS

The mortise lock, as the name implies, is fitted into the door stile as if it were a tenon. Mark the top and the bottom of the lock on the end of the door and accurately mark the position of the keyhole on both

sides of it. Cut the mortise for the lock in the usual way, boring out most of the waste with a twist bit and finishing with a mortise chisel. These locks may be purchased for both deep and narrow stiles, the narrow stile being used mostly for glazed doors. Care must be taken in positioning the lock not to cut into the door tenon, as this will weaken the door considerably. For security, the lock plate which fits on the door jamb and receives the lock should also be of the mortise type and not simply a flat plate.

CUPBOARD LOCKS

A cupboard lock is recessed into the inside of the door stile and is usually handed. Mark out and drill for the key before recessing the body of the lock. The key escutcheon plate is the only part which will show on the outside of the door and the

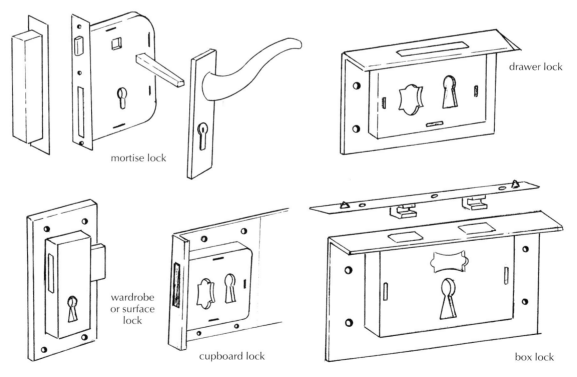

mortise lock

drawer lock

wardrobe or surface lock

cupboard lock

box lock

Various types of lock.

position of this is often the most important consideration.

DRAWER LOCKS

The drawer lock is much the same as the cupboard lock except for the fact that the key fits in an upright rather than a sideways manner. Some locks are made with two key openings so that they may be used for both cupboards and drawers.

SURFACE OR WARDROBE LOCKS

The surface lock is screwed on to the inside of the door direct and the keyhole is cut to suit. These locks will suit either a left- or a right-hand situation.

BOX LOCKS

The box lock comes with a separate link plate and may be of either a recess or a mortise form. The lock is fitted to the base of the box first, then the link plate is locked in place in the lock and the lid of the box closed on to it. The link plate has two prongs which project up and mark the position of the plate on the underside of the box lid. The plate is then released from the lock and positioned on the box lid, with the prongs in position. Mark round the plate and cut it in flush.

CASTORS

SCREW CASTORS

The screw castor, as its name implies, fastens into the bottom of a furniture leg with a large steel screw. A hole must be drilled in the leg slightly less than the diameter of the screw. The castor is screwed in place by placing a nail punch into one of the holes in the base plate of the castor and turning it, while gripping the castor wheel and the

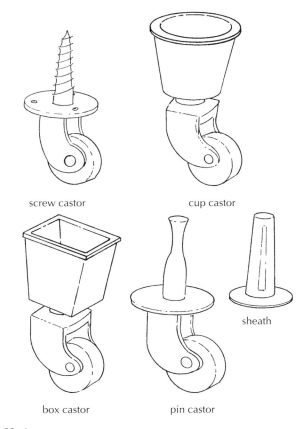

screw castor   cup castor

sheath

box castor   pin castor

Various castors.

nail punch together. Sometimes a small screw or wire nail is put in the hole in the plate to prevent the screw from coming loose. These castors may be purchased with either brass or china wheels. Castor rings are available which fit over the ends of legs and help to prevent the ends from splitting. Unfortunately, these rings are all to often regarded as being ornamental only and are not used.

PIN CASTORS

The pin castor is similar to the screw castor except that instead of a steel screw it has a steel pin which fits into a metal sheath. The end of the furniture leg is drilled out to take the sheath and the castor pin is then driven into it.

CUP AND BOX CASTORS

Cup castors fit on the ends of turned legs and box castors on the ends of square ones. The end of the leg is cut and shaped to fit into the castor which is then secured with screws.

NOTES ON FITTING DOORS

The usual procedure for fitting hinges, locks or any other door furniture is to fit all the metalwork before any painting or polishing is carried out. The fittings are then removed and refitted, with new screws, after the door has polished or painted. Allowance should be made in fitting doors which are exposed to the weather because they will tend to swell in wet and shrink in dry conditions. A door which is fitted close in warm summer weather will be much too tight in winter. Therefore all doors and other working parts should fit correctly in damp weather, and open or slack fitting must be tolerated in warm, dry conditions.

It must be remembered that all structural work will settle slightly over time and that doors will be the first to show this movement. Any door which is fitted with very little clearance at the bottom will soon need adjusting there, whereas the top will never become tight. This should be remembered when positioning hinges. In the vertical joints, a door will tend to open on the hinge side at the top but will remain constant at the bottom hinge. On the lock side of the door the vertical joint will remain constant at the bottom but tend to become tight at the top. The sagging of the door will also affect the positioning of the lock, which will need adjustment if insufficient allowance is made when fitting.

Sometimes the effects of sagging are made worse because the door has a heavy glass panel or mirror, as is the case with some wardrobe doors. The effect of the weight of the panel may be alleviated to a large extent by the careful placement of packing. The weight needs to be concentrated away from the most vulnerable places. It can be seen from the illustration below that the weight is best distributed so that the force is as near the hinge side as possible at the bottom of the door and near the top joint on the outer side. This is accomplished by making sure that the glass touches the frame only at these points.

Doors sometimes warp slightly so that they no longer fit properly against the stops and some pressure may need to be applied for the lock to catch. It is practically impossible to correct the warp in a door and so the best remedy is to remove and refit the doorstops to suit.

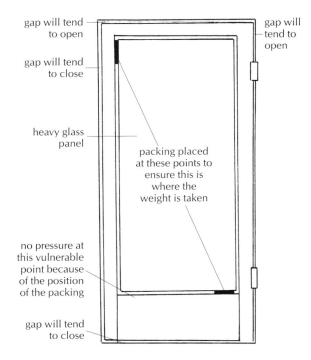

Weight distributed to best advantage.

14

Veneering

Veneered work has been frowned upon in some quarters, no doubt because of the assumption that veneering is used to cover up shoddy and inferior work, and, in fairness, this has happened in the past. In proper use, however, veneers are laid only on good, solid timber which has been properly prepared and worked. Veneer is used when the cost of using solid timber would be prohibitive, or when curl or figured wood is required for effect and would be unsatisfactory in solid timber. Another 'proper' use of veneer is in connection with curved work, when its building up in layers is required and its appearance would be unsightly without veneering.

Veneers themselves come in two types: saw cut and knife cut. Originally, of course, all veneers were saw cut by hand and could be ¼in (6mm) or more thick. Later on, with the introduction of machinery, thinner veneers could be cut and later still the present method of slicing veneers with a knife was introduced that enabled veneers to be cut very thinly indeed.

There are two different methods of laying veneer: 'hand' and 'caul' veneering. The first is done with a veneering hammer and the second with a press or caul. Both methods call for the proper selection and preparation of the groundwork.

GROUNDWORK

SOLID TIMBER

If you are laying your veneer on solid wood it is best to cut the wood into strips and to re-glue them, reversing every other one in order to prevent warping. If this is not done you should always lay the veneer on the side of the timber which was nearer the heartwood as this will help to counteract the natural tendency for the wood to warp so that the heartwood presents itself on the convex. You can determine the side of the heartwood by examining the end of the board: the annual growth rings will show which side was nearer the centre of the tree.

Other problems which may need to be dealt with are knots, and in the case of salvaged timber, old nails or nail holes. Any defect is best cut out and replaced with similar wood, with the grain in the same direction. The surface should then be gone over with a toothing plane to give an extra key for the glue and to ensure that the surface is completely flat. Clean the surface with a vacuum cleaner in order to remove all dust.

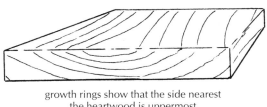

growth rings show that the side nearest the heartwood is uppermost

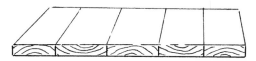

when veneering it is best to cut the wood into strips and to re-glue with every other piece turned over

Veneer should be laid on the side nearest to the heartwood.

123

When veneering on curved work a certain amount of end grain will be involved, and it will be necessary to treat this with a size, a solution of dilute glue. The size is applied after the groundwork has been planed with the toothing plane and should be thin enough to soak in and not need sanding or replaning after it is dry. Making sure that the size is of the right consistency, so that it soaks in but is thick enough to do the job, requires some trial and error on a waste piece of the same timber.

VENEERING ON CHIPBOARD

If you are working on chipboard the surface will have to be treated with size and the edges will have to be lipped with solid wood before the veneering. Veneering both sides is recommended to prevent any tendency to bow.

BLOCKBOARD AND PLYWOOD

Both these boards will have to have their edges lipped with solid wood before veneering can begin and can be treated in the same way as chipboard, although there is less of a tendency for bowing when only one side is veneered.

MDF

MDF may have its edges lipped or they may be moulded, stained and coloured to match the veneer, although this would not be done on high-class work.

VENEER

The veneer itself will need some preparation before being laid, and it may be advisable to get this under way before preparing the groundwork, because the veneer may have to be left overnight. Some veneers, such as curl and figure, will have to be flat-tened before their use. This is done by wiping the veneer with a slightly damp cloth and placing it between flat boards with paper on either side of the veneer and a weight on top, so that the veneer dries properly and flat. The veneer must be laid soon after it is removed from between the boards or it will lose its flatness. Care must be taken not to get the veneer more than damp and not to allow it to become cold, a comfortable room temperature is satisfactory.

HAMMER VENEERING

Laying veneer with a hammer is suitable only for knife-cut veneer, and only on relatively small pieces of work. Large panels and tabletops are best done by the caul method along with any marquetry or other work with a number of joints.

Let us assume that we are laying one piece of knife-cut veneer on a small panel. The panel will have been cut and planed to size and toothed ready for veneering. The tools required are a veneering hammer, an iron, a craft knife, the glue pot and a supply of hot water and clean rags.

Preparing the Glue

Scotch glue is purchased in cake or pearl form and is dissolved in hot water, in a special glue pot. The pot itself has two compartments: an outer one containing hot water and an inner one that contains the glue. Place a quantity of glue in the inner container and cover it with a little cold water. Fill the outer container about two-thirds full of water and place on a heat source, with the inner pot in place. Bring almost to the point of boiling. Some glue pots have a couple of holes in them to allow the steam to escape, with others it will be necessary to place some small blocks of wood between the lips of the pots to raise the inner one, allow steam to escape and prevent the outer pot from boiling over. Keep stirring the glue, adding more water if required, and keep on the heat. When the glue is ready a film or crust will form and the glue should then be tested for thickness. Pick up some glue on the glue brush and allow it to fall back into the pot, it should run in a continuous stream with no lumps or thick parts and it should not break up into droplets. Add more water if required.

Knife-cut veneers have a right and a wrong side when it comes to laying them. They have a face or tight side and a loose or tension side. In general, veneers are laid loose side down, and the way to determine which side is which is to rub the veneer against the side of your face. You should thereby be able to tell the smooth side from the more rough, loose, tension side. Remember that the tight side should be up for gluing.

The groundwork and all the tools that are likely to come into contact with the veneer or glue should be made warm before starting, and it is imperative when working with Scotch glue to keep everything hot and to work quickly, and so make sure before starting that you have everything on hand.

Spread an even layer of glue over the groundwork and position the veneer on top. Moisten the top surface of the veneer

with a hot, damp rag and put a few dabs of glue on top of the veneer to act as a lubricant for the veneering hammer. With one hand on its handle to guide and the other one putting pressure over the blade, begin squeezing the excess of glue out from under the veneer, starting in the centre and working towards the edges.

If the glue becomes stiff or cold apply heat with the iron, taking care not to burn the veneer. The hammer must be pulled across the surface, from the centre to an edge, at an angle across the grain and excessive glue should be cleaned off with a hot, damp rag. Do not get the surface too wet or the veneer could lift.

Have a good look at the top surface to make sure that the glue has been removed and run your hand over the surface to feel for any blisters or bubbles. If any area is suspect tap on it with your finger nail and you will be able to tell by the feel and the noise that it makes whether or not the veneer is secure. If the veneer is not stuck down apply a little heat with the iron and hammer it down, using a little glue as a lubricant once again. If this does not rectify the situation you will have to slice the veneer at this point with a craft knife, cutting with the grain. Lift the veneer very carefully and insert some fresh glue and hammer down the veneer, this time squeezing the glue towards the split just made. When the veneer is flat again glue a piece of brown paper over the split in the veneer.

When the veneer is laid and stood aside to dry the air should be kept away from the surface by placing it face down on a flat, clean surface. If more than one panel has been prepared they may be placed face to face for drying, with some paper between them to prevent any possibility of their sticking together.

Knife-cut veneer may quite successfully be hammer-laid on curved surfaces, provided that the curve is not too severe; but remember that end grain will need to be sized.

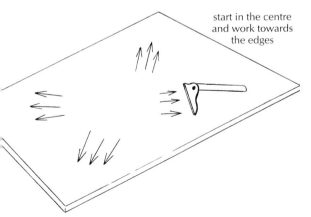

start in the centre and work towards the edges

Work the glue away from the centre and towards the edge.

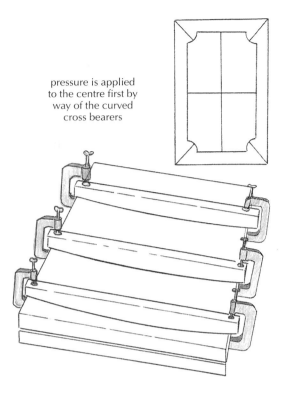

pressure is applied to the centre first by way of the curved cross bearers

The caul.

THE CAUL METHOD (HOT GLUE)

The caul method is employed when patterns are involved, as with the door panel shown above, or for laying saw-cut veneers.

The caul itself is simply a flat board which is made hot and cramped over veneer between cross bearers. The caul needs to be just a little larger in size than the size of the panel being veneered and may be made of solid timber, although MDF is satisfactory, being readily available in perfectly flat boards. The real secret with this method is in the cross bearers, which are made from 2in (5cm) thick timbers and are slightly rounded on the underside. It may be seen from the illustration that having the cross bearers rounded means that, when the cramps are tightened, pressure is applied to the centre first and then to the whole area.

Let us first look at a panel which is being veneered with a single sheet of veneer on one side. The panel will be prepared as before and a caul of MDF cut just over size. Next cross bearers must be cut that will reach across the full width of the caul; these bearers need to be placed 6 to 8in (16 to 20cm) apart, above and below the work.

The bearers have to be rounded on the bottom, and the best way of doing this is to find the centre of one pair and place a small piece of wood between the bearers at this point, with a cramp at each end. Tighten up the cramps so that the bearers become bent as shown below. Place a straight edge against the side of the bearers and mark a line as shown. Remove the

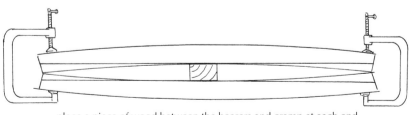

place a piece of wood between the bearers and cramp at each end

plane away the waste wood so that the bearers are curved on the bottom

Marking the bearers.

cramps and plane the bottoms of the bearers to the line so that they are curved.

First cover the groundwork with an even layer of glue and put this on one side to dry; the glue is considered dry when it is possible to place a hand on the glued surface and then to take it away without its sticking in any way. Next, prepare all the cross bearers and have all the cramps open to the correct amount; when the time comes it will be necessary to work very quickly, so everything needs to be prepared and on hand. Place the panel on top of the bottom cross bearers and carefully position the veneer in place. This will need to be secured in place with a couple of veneer pins. The caul now needs to be heated through and hot enough so that you cannot bear to put your hand on it. It is also a good idea to heat the cramps and cross bearers to some extent to prevent their taking heat from the caul when they come into contact with it. Now, working as quickly as possible, place the heated caul over the veneer, put the top cross bearers in position and tighten the cramps, beginning with the middle one and working out to the ends, then retighten the cramps again. The heat from the caul will now melt the glue and it must be stood aside for from twelve to twenty-four hours before the cramps are removed.

THE PRESS METHOD (COLD GLUE)

The press and caul methods are identical except for the fact that in the press method nothing requires heating. The veneer, groundwork and cross bearers are all made and treated in exactly the same way.

DECORATIVE DESIGNS IN VENEERS

If more than just one piece of veneer is to be laid in order to make a pattern, such as the door front shown overleaf, then the hammer-laying of the veneer is not possible and the caul or press method must be employed. The pattern must first be drawn on a piece of strong cartridge paper, which is laid flat and pinned into position on a flat board. Veneers can be purchased in a flitch; that is, the veneers are kept in the same order that they were in when cut from the log. This means that the grain of each piece varies hardly at all from that of the piece next to it and decorative patterns may be made from them in the following ways:

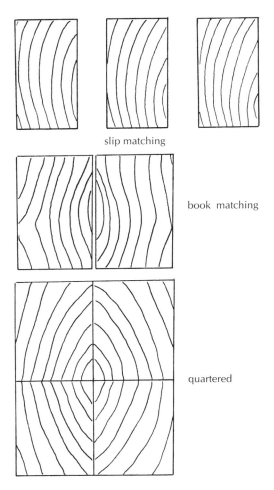

slip matching

book matching

quartered

Veneer sheet arranged to form patterns.

- slip matching: this simply means taking a number of sequential sheets and slipping them sideways for joining;
- book matching: pairs of veneers are opened as if one were opening the pages of a book;
- quartered: the first two sequential sheets are open as are the pages of a book; the second two are opened in the same way but are flipped over on their horizontal axis.

For our example shown opposite, take four sequential sheets and open them as for quartering. With saw-cut veneer the edges to be joined must be shot on a shooting board and then the pieces must be cut and planed to size, so that they fit exactly on to the paper pattern.

If knife-cut veneers are used the veneers may be slightly overlapped where they join; a straight edge is positioned on the joint and both veneers cut through with a marquetry knife or a veneer saw. The waste veneer is removed and the joint taped together with veneer tape. The two panels are then cut to size, once again using the straight edge.

Now the hollow corners need to be cut. These may be marked for cutting with a pair of compasses and, in the case of knife-cut veneer, cut carefully with a marquetry knife. Saw-cut veneers will have to be cut with a fine fret saw, and it may be advisable to place the veneers together so that all four corners can be cut together. After being cut they are cleaned up with a fine file or with a piece of rounded wood with fine sandpaper wound round it.

The veneers cut so far are now glued to the paper pattern with Cow gum. The pattern we are using as an example has a black line between the centre veneers and the outer crossbanding. These lines can be purchased in a number of sizes and woods from veneer suppliers. The lines placed in the hollow corners will need to be steamed in order to keep their shape. This is done by cutting a piece of wood to the same radius as the corners, steaming a section of line, taping one end to the wood and gradually bending it around the radius, taping it in place as you go. Leave the line in place until it is dry, by which time it will be possible to remove the tape and the line will hold its shape enough to easily be glued on to the design and held in place with veneer tape. Position one such corner and mitre the ends where they join the straight pieces. Continue with the other corners and then fit the straight lines. Cut the crossbanding and glue into position on the paper design. The whole may now be glued into position on the groundwork, paper-side up, and placed in the press until the glue is dry. To ensure that the pattern is glued to the groundwork square and in the correct position, crosshairs are drawn dividing the panel into four. Similar crosshairs are drawn on the groundwork and these are lined up for gluing. When the panel is removed from the press the paper design is removed with a little warm water and the veneers can be cleaned up with a cabinet scraper and sandpaper.

VENEERING WITH IMPACT ADHESIVE

It is possible to lay veneers quite successfully with impact adhesives, and, indeed, this may be the best method to employ for marquetry or other intricate joins. The adhesive is applied with a toothed spreader to both of the surfaces to be joined and allowed to become touch-dry, that is to say, that it should be possible to touch the glue with a finger without feeling any stickiness at all. When the surfaces are brought into contact they will adhere instantly and so great care must be taken in positioning the veneer. One way that may be used is to place a piece of paper between the surfaces; the paper will not stick and the veneer can be positioned accurately above the ground-work. Once the veneer is in position the paper can be carefully slid out from beneath the veneer and the veneers pressed down. A roller may be used to ensure that the veneer is in firm contact all over.

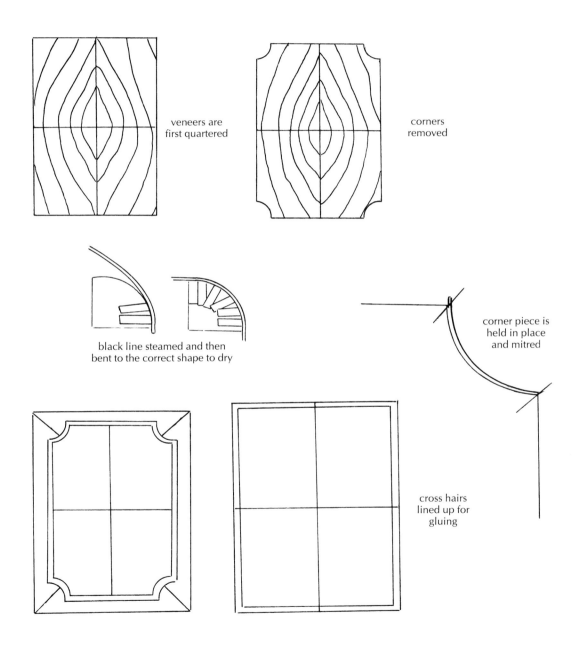

veneers are
first quartered

corners
removed

black line steamed and then
bent to the correct shape to dry

corner piece is
held in place
and mitred

cross hairs
lined up for
gluing

Decorative door panel.

15

Wood Turning

The lathe is unique among woodworking machines in that it yields results unachievable by any other method. All other woodworking machines are designed to do a job previously done by hand. The lathe itself consists of four basic parts: the headstock, which holds one end of the work and is responsible for its rotation, the tailstock, which simply supports the other end of the work, the bed of the lathe, and the tool rest.

Remember that a revolving piece of wood is far more dangerous to work on than a stationary one. The chisel should be held firmly, and the work approached with caution; if the chisel is forced out of position it may cause damage to the work and, more importantly, to the worker. Never wear loose or ill-fitting clothing which could get caught in the moving bits, and always wear safety glasses or goggles.

Sharp tools are, as always, very important, and in turning they can be used in one of two ways, either for cutting or scraping. Turning chisels are generally long and stout with long handles to give plenty of leverage. In use, the chisel is held firmly on the tool rest, which has been positioned as close to the work as possible and a little above the centre line of the work. Some workers will hold the chisel with the thumb

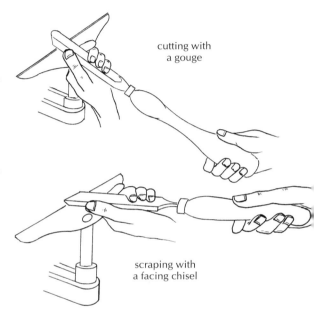

Scraping and cutting on the lathe.

of the left hand on top and the fingers below, pressed up against the tool rest. The other hand holds the end of the handle and controls the angle at which the chisel meets the work. Another way of holding the chisel is to rest the palm of the hand on top of the chisel over the tool rest. Both

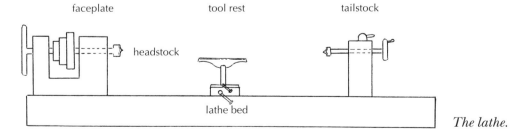

The lathe.

methods are suitable and you must decide which feels the more natural for you.

THE TOOLS

Most work on the lathe can be carried out with a set of chisels comprising a couple of differently sized gouges, a side chisel and a round-nose chisel. A diamond point and a facing chisel are also useful. There are, of course, many different types and sizes of chisel available, some of which are very specialized and the turner will gradually build up his own collection. Some experienced workers even grind down old files to make their own chisels.

The gouge is the only tool used exclusively for cutting. It is held with the handle lower than the point and approaches the work near the top with a lateral movement to right or left, the movement being towards the side on which the shaving is being cut. The gouge is ground on the out-side, but, unlike the ordinary firmer gouge, it is ground back more on the sides.

The side chisel may be used in a similar way to the gouge on work of small or moderate diameter, but on larger diameters is better used in a scraping manner.

In scraping, the chisel approaches the work more or less level with the centre of it. This is because the upper point must not be allowed to come into contact with the surface or it could dig in with disastrous results. The main use of the side chisel is for parting and making incisions. These incisions are made a little at a time so that the shavings are forced away by the wedge-like shape. The chisel is moved slightly sideways each time until there is sufficient clearance for the chisel to go as deep as required.

THE TOOL REST

Turning tools cannot be used without a rest or support. The work revolves towards the

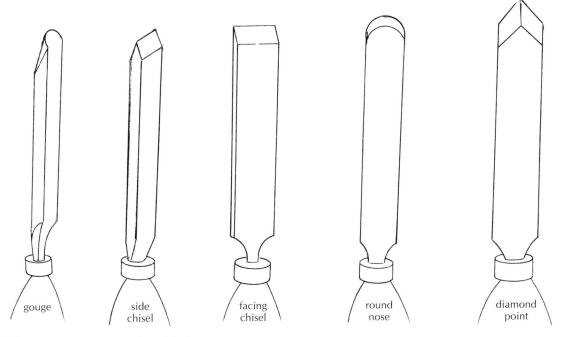

The most common turning chisels.

gouge side chisel facing chisel round nose diamond point

operator and the rest should be positioned as near to the cutting edge of the chisel as possible. If the rest is set too far back there will be an extra stress on the chisel and it will be more difficult to take an even shaving of wood. The rest can be adjusted for height and angle as well as distance from the work, but, in practice, the height is seldom adjusted. For turning between centres the rest is set just above the centre line of the work. For faceplate turning the rest is often set in line with or very slightly below the centre when turning the actual face of the work, and raised just above the centre for turning the edge.

FORK CENTRES AND CHUCKS

The fork centre is the most usual way of securing the end of the wood to the headstock. It comes in various sizes according to the work being undertaken and either screw on to the headstock or have a tapered shank that fits into a hole in the stock. Generally speaking, the fork centre is tapped into place in the end of the wood and then the whole assembly is attached to the lathe. The other end of the work is then held by the dead centre in the tailstock. With most lathes the dead centre is made so that it revolves with the work; if this is not the case it may be lubricated with a little light oil or candle grease.

With some larger work the fork centre may not be secure enough and either a cup chuck or four-jaw chuck may be used. These two chucks are also of use for turning small items such as eggcups which need to be turned at the end as well as along the side.

PREPARING THE WOOD

Choose your wood carefully, checking for knots and defects which could cause trouble during the turning. When preparing the work for turning between centres, cut the wood to the required length, allowing a little waste at each end. Mark the centre at each end, either by drawing lines across the diagonals or by setting a marking gauge to about half the wood thickness and marking from all sides. It is always best to mark the centre in this way rather than to guess its position. Guessing may result in the work's failure to hold up to diameter. Make a saw cut at one end to take the fork centre and plane off as much waste timber as is practicable before placing the work on the lathe.

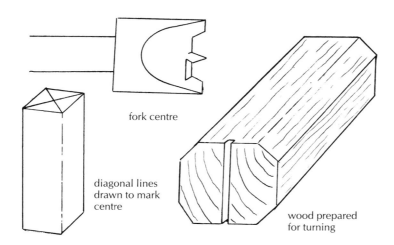

fork centre

diagonal lines drawn to mark centre

wood prepared for turning

Timber prepared for turning.

When turning between centres, the length of the wood is usually longer than the diameter, but this does not mean that the finished article is always so. Sometimes it is beneficial to turn a number of small, similar items in a stick and to cut them to length after sanding or polishing.

If the item to be turned has a greater diameter than its length it is better to have the grain running the other way and to turn it on the faceplate.

When the work is on the lathe the first thing to be done is to turn it round. This is accomplished with the gouge and the diameter should be checked regularly with callipers. Once the wood is perfectly round with no flat spots the position of the several features of the turning can be marked. Turn the thicker parts first and always work from a high point to a low, never the other way round; even when performing the turning you must work in the direction of the grain.

When turning coving mark the starting point with a parting tool and then use a gouge, rolling the bevel down into the cove, always working from high to low. When turning beads use a side chisel and work from the centre of the bead, rolling the chisel sideways down to the base of the bead on each side. When turning a straight taper, callipers are used to check the large and the small diameter at each end, which are turned first. The wood between these two points is then removed, first with a gouge and then finished with a side chisel, all the time checking for straightness with a small straight edge or the blade of a try square.

FACEPLATE TURNING

Some items, such as bowls, cannot be turned between centres and in these cases the wood is first roughly cut to size and then secured on the faceplate, which is itself then secured to the headstock. In the case of a bowl, its top would be fixed to the

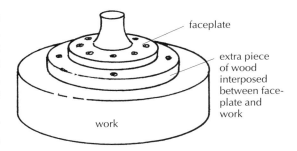

The faceplate.

faceplate first, so that the outside of the bowl can be turned; when this has been completed the faceplate can be secured to the base of the bowl and the interior turned out.

The simple faceplate itself is a round disc of metal, usually cast, which screws on to the lathe mandrel and has screw holes in it through which the wood is secured. The faceplate screws on to the mandrel in such a way that the act of turning will tend to tighten rather than loosen it. Sometimes the work is secured to the faceplate direct, but more commonly another piece of wood is interposed. Care must be taken when fixing the work to the plate that the screws do not go into an area of the work which will be removed during turning. To avoid this problem it is possible to glue the work to the faceplate instead. One piece of wood is screwed to the faceplate as usual and the work is then glued to this wood, with a sheet or two of newspaper between to aid separation when the work is complete.

MAKING MEASUREMENTS ON THE LATHE

Callipers are by far the most common means of measuring work on the lathe. They can be set to the diameter of a piece being copied or they can be set to a particular measurement against a rule. On very small diameters tests with callipers can be made while the lathe is still running; but generally it is better to stop the lathe for callipering the work. When faceplate-turning the diameter can be checked direct with a rule. To check the diameter accurately, one end of the rule is held flush with one side of the work with the forefinger and the other end is moved in a slight arc so that it passes to and fro over the centre of the circle. The full diameter may then be noted.

When checking the size and shape of contours on the lathe it is often useful to have a template to use in conjunction with the callipers. It is frequently necessary to check not just the diameter of a particular contour but also its shape and distance from some other feature on the turning. The template may be made of card or thick paper, depending on the template size, and can be held against the work. The template does not have to be of the entire article being turned; it is often more convenient to have templates of small sections of the item.

GENERAL TURNING

In turning, as much as in general woodwork, it is necessary to work in the direction of the grain. Thus, in the case of a tapered item, the chisel must always cut from the larger diameter to the smaller. Similarly when turning beads and roundels the cutting must progress from the large to the small diameter.

When using the gouge to turn down from a large to a small diameter the tool is best held on its side rather than flat with the work. With faceplate- and cup-chuck-turning it is best to turn out the small diameters entirely with a scraping tool, with either a chisel, if the bottom of the item is flat, or a round-nose if the bottom is curved.

When the work is completely finished it is customary to remove it from the lathe by turning down to the smallest possible diameter without its breaking and then sawing the final bit.

BUILT-UP WORK

Work which is to be turned on the lathe does not have to be made out of a solid individual piece, it can be built up from several parts. The chief reasons for doing this are, first, so that a large diameter can be turned without the work's being too heavy or liable to shrink too much in one direction, and, secondly, for decorative effect. As an example of the former, a hexagonal or octagonal, hollow pillar can be prepared with filler pieces at each end

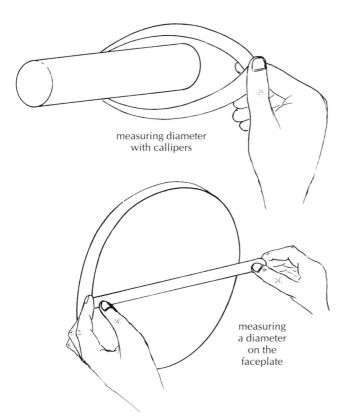

measuring diameter
with callipers

measuring
a diameter
on the
faceplate

Checking dimensions on the lathe.

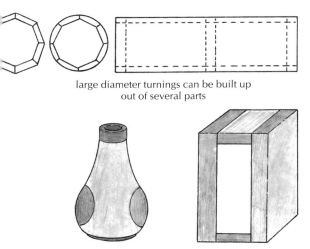

large diameter turnings can be built up
out of several parts

Work built up for decorative effect.

for the centres, and of the second, differently coloured woods can be joined together to make patterns when turned.

SPIRAL TURNING

Most spiral turnings are now made on an automatic lathe; but if this equipment is not available a description of the traditional method may be of use.

The spiral turning is really a combination of lathe work and carving, an example of which is shown right. First, the wood is cut and planed square, as for any leg, and is then centred on the lathe. The spiral section of the leg is turned to its maximum diameter, and the foot and necks are turned. The necks are turned to the same depth as it is intended to cut the twist. The next job is to set out the spiral and, as can be seen from the drawing, the single twist begins and ends on opposite sides of the turning. This means that, when calculating the number of twists required, you will count so many twists-and-a-half. In the example shown there are four-and-a-half twists between the points A and B. To set out this spiral, divide the circumference by four equidistant, longitudinal lines. Multiply the number of twists required by four and divide the length of the cylinder by the product (eighteen). Spin pencil lines round the cylinder at these points. Make a flexible straight edge by folding a piece of stout paper; this will give you a firm edge to rule by. Using the straight edge and beginning at A, rule a continuous diagonal line across the divisions until B is reached, forming a left-handed spiral. If two more lines are drawn, one on either side of the first, the setting-out will be complete. It is usual to cut twists in pairs, one left-handed and one right-handed, so that a table with four legs would have two of each. To set out the right-handed twist a beginning is made at the same point and the line is carried round in the opposite direction. To cut the spiral, a piece of masking tape is placed on each side of the tenon saw to mark the depth of the spiral and the outer lines are cut down to the tape. A carver's gouge is now used to remove the waste wood between the saw cuts, leaving a rounded bottom. A chisel is then used to round the top of the spiral, after which the whole item is finally shaped with a file and coarse sandpaper.

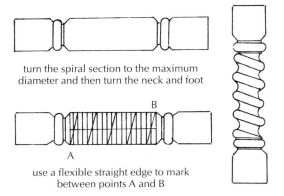

turn the spiral section to the maximum
diameter and then turn the neck and foot

use a flexible straight edge to mark
between points A and B

Making a spiral.

16

Power Tools and Machinery

ELECTRIC DRILLS

There must be very many different electric drills on the market these days, making it difficult to choose the one that best suits you. A small, single-speed drill is cheap to buy but not very versatile. Choose a drill which has a variable-speed trigger; this is an advantage when starting some holes, and a hammer-action option. Builders will want a powerful drill, with hammer action if they are continually drilling masonry; other site workers may feel that a cordless, battery-powered drill is ideal, but must bear in mind that a battery-powered drill will not be as powerful as a mains one. Another useful item is the keyless chuck, which makes for the quick and efficient changing of drill or screwdriver bits and eliminates the problem of where to best keep the chuck key. You will probably find that you use your drill a good deal and it is worth spending a little extra to get a powerful, variable-speed tool with a large chuck, be it mains or battery powered.

Remember too, that there are now many useful attachments available for electric drills, including sanding, turning and sawing tools, and a powerful, variable-speed drill is required for these. One useful adjunct is a drill stand which holds the body of the drill firmly in a vertical position for accurate drilling. A mortising attachment may also be purchased to go with the stand. This is a square, hollow chisel with an auger bit in the centre. In use, the auger bit cuts away the bulk of the wood and the square chisel cleans down

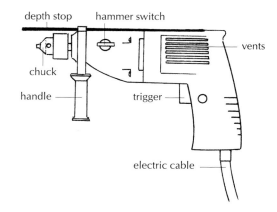

The electric drill.

the sides of the hole, forming a neat, square hole. The wood is then moved along a little and the operation repeated to form a mortise.

SANDERS

For a small workshop, rather than a large, industrial one, small disc, orbital or belt sanders may be considered. Belt sanders are generally better than orbital ones, which tend to leave little circular marks on the surface of the work if the paper becomes clogged. However, they do have a tendency to leave lines on the work. Disc sanders have all the bad points of the other two. In short, if you must use a mechanical sander, take care, use fine paper and make sure that you get one that has a dustbag fitted. Electric sanders are fine for work that is to be painted, but fine cabinet work should always be finished by hand.

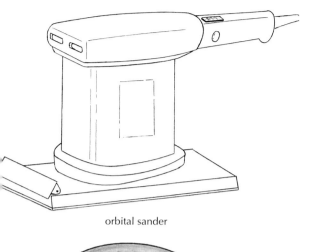

orbital sander

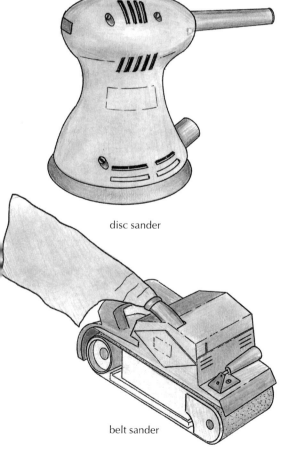

disc sander

belt sander

Various electric sanders.

THE ROUTER

The router is another very versatile power tool which may be used for moulding, shaping, cutting rebates, grooving and jointing. There is now a wide range of cutters and jigs on the market, ranging from one- and two-flute groove cutters, moulding and cove cutters, dovetail cutters and jigs, to attachments for spiral turning. The router operates at a very high speed, which means that ordinary high-speed cutters burn easily and it is best to buy the more expensive tungsten-tipped type. The high operating speed also means that the cutter takes a long time to stop rotating after it has been switched off and it should never be started up with the cutter in contact with wood.

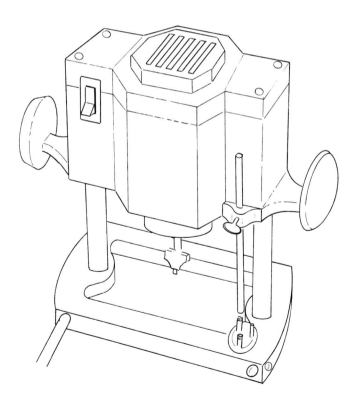

Electric router.

137

Most routers come with an adjustable fence for following straight edges and a facility for following internal curves, together with a depth gauge and plunge facility. Some cutters have a stylus that allows them to follow a shaped edge, enabling even intricate shapes to be moulded. The dovetail cutter and jig is another worthwhile purchase, enabling slot and drawer dovetails to be cut with little effort.

There are several ways in which a router may be used. Following a straight edge for rebating is done by using the router's own fence, but when grooves have to be cut towards the middle of the work the fence will often not reach. In this case a batten will have to be pinned or cramped in place for the router to follow. To calculate the amount of offset required between the groove and the batten, measure the width of the router base, subtract the diameter of the cutter and halve the result. If the base of the router is 160mm (6.3in) in width and the cutter is 20mm (0.8in) in diameter, the offset will be 70mm (2.8in).

Most routers will have some form of template guide that will allow shapes to be followed. The router will follow around the inside or the outside of a shape cut out of a plywood sheet. If it is to follow the inside of the shape, the shape cut out will have to be larger than the actual size required in order to allow for the offset of the template guide or follower. The reverse is true, that is, that the shape will have to be smaller than required if the router is to follow around the outside. The difference in size will be equal to half the difference between the diameter of the router cutter and the diameter of the guide. If you are following the inside of a template and the diameter of the guide is 50mm (2in) and the diameter of the router cutter is 20mm (0.8in) then the template will have to be 15mm (0.6in) larger than the actual size required.

Sometimes it will be necessary to cut a groove on the narrow edge of a piece of wood and in those circumstances it is best to cramp another piece of wood alongside the edge in order to give a wider platform

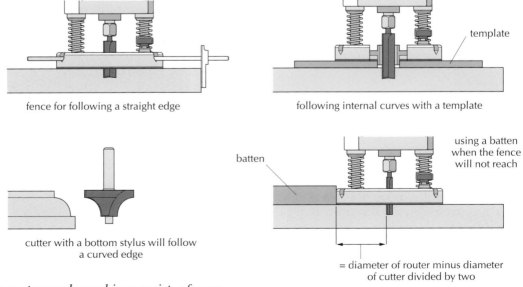

fence for following a straight edge

following internal curves with a template

template

cutter with a bottom stylus will follow a curved edge

batten

using a batten when the fence will not reach

= diameter of router minus diameter of cutter divided by two

The router can be used in a variety of ways.

The jigsaw.

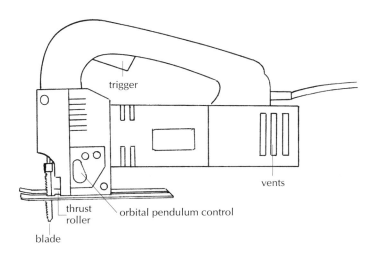

trigger

vents

thrust roller

orbital pendulum control

blade

for the router. Another way is to invest in an edge cutter where the router itself will still run on the face of the board.

The router may also be used for very accurate drilling. The hole obtained will always be exactly perpendicular to the surface and the hole will be much cleaner than that made by a drill. The perfect example is when fitting plugs over the top of hidden screws. A two-flute cutter is used in the router to countersink the screw hole and then a plug cutter of corresponding size is used, again in the router, to cut the plug. The result, if matching wood has been used, is an almost invisible plug.

SAWS

THE JIGSAW

The jigsaw is a useful tool to have on site or in any workshop. Its primary use is for cutting shapes, but it may be used for ripping and crosscutting timber if required. Again it is well worth spending a little extra on purchasing one of the better machines with a pendulum action. The blade does not just move up and down when cutting, but away from the work on the downward,

non-cutting stroke and towards the work on the upward cutting stroke. This makes for a cleaner and quicker cut and imposes less work on the saw.

When using a jigsaw it is important to remember that it cuts on the upward stroke, and so the cleaner cut will be on the bottom. Whenever possible mark out the work on the side which will not show when the job is completed and cut from that side. The upward cutting stroke also means that sawdust is thrown up and so goggles or safety glasses are essential. Be aware at all times that the part of the blade that is underneath the work is exposed and unprotected; it is also important from the safety point of view to allow the blade to come to a complete stop before removing it from the work, any failure to do so will result in damage to both the work and the blade, and maybe even to the operator. A variety of blades are available for cutting wood, laminates, plastics and metals.

THE BANDSAW

The bandsaw is used for cutting outside shapes and for ripping down thick timbers that cannot be handled on the circular saw. Such saws may be purchased with two or

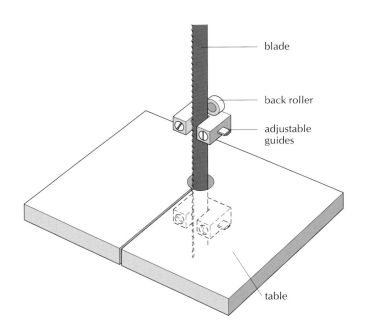

blade

back roller

adjustable
guides

table

The bandsaw blade will have guides above and below the table.

three wheels; the three-wheels version being more expensive but generally having a bigger throat, which means that larger shapes can be dealt with. The drawback to bandsaws is that they cannot cut a truly straight line; the guides that are supplied are generally of little help and the best way of cutting straight is to mark and follow a pencil line. The blade runs through some adjustable guides, above and below the table on the better machines.

When fitting a new blade to a machine make sure that the power supply is turned off, slip the new blade over the wheels and tighten the top adjustable wheel enough to hold it in place. More tension is then applied by raising the top blade further; sufficient tension is needed to prevent the blade from slipping. Manufacturers' guidelines on tensioning should be supplied with the saw. Slowly rotate the bottom wheel by hand to check that the blade runs near enough in the centre of the wheels without wandering to the front or the back. If the blade does wander, this can be corrected with an adjustment wheel at the back, which cants the top wheel. Turn this adjustment,

while manually rotating the bottom wheel, until the blade runs true. Adjustment may now be made of the guides to the rear and the sides of the blade. The side guides are adjusted so that they are as close to the blade as possible, allowing the blade to run freely between them, and set far enough back as not to interfere with the set of the teeth. The guide at the back of the blade usually takes the form of a small roller and is set just clear of the back of the blade so that the blade touches it during cutting but runs freely when not under pressure.

Always have the blade guard set as low as possible when cutting; there should be just enough blade showing between the top of the work and the bottom of the guard to see any pencil line which is being followed as the wood is cut. When cutting curves use a thin blade and avoid twisting. Keep your eye on the line just in front of the blade and make sure that this line is being fed into the blade from the front and not approaching from the side. With intricate shapes it is a good idea to cut out roughly at first to remove the bulk of the waste and then to cut out accurately to the line afterwards. On tight or long curves where there is a danger of the blade's binding, a series of straight cuts should first be made from the outside of the waste, down to the line, at intervals around the curve. In this way the cut is divided up into a series of smaller ones.

Most of the blades used today by the DIY enthusiast will be of the hardened type, which are simply disposed of when they become blunt. However, a much better and cleaner cut is obtained from a conventional blade which can be sharpened by hand. To sharpen a blade a special wooden vice is made (*see* below) to hold it securely over about one-quarter of its circumference at a time. Cut two pieces of wood, one for either side of the bandsaw blade. One piece should be about 100mm (4in) wide and the other about 200mm (8in) so that it may be fitted into the vice. Chamfer the tops and drill through both pieces so that a large dowel may be inserted at each end.

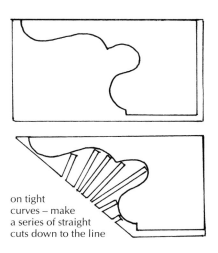

on tight
curves – make
a series of straight
cuts down to the line

Cutting intricate shapes.

The dowel is glued into one piece only and left free in the other.

To use, the two sections are separated just enough to insert the blade with the

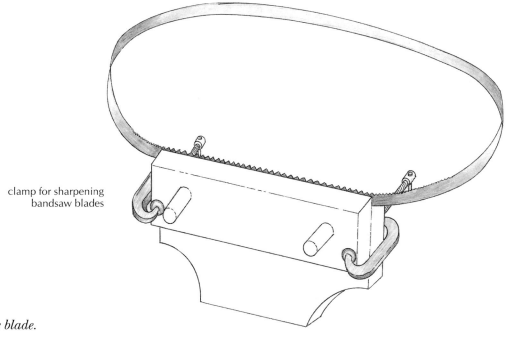

clamp for sharpening
bandsaw blades

Sharpening the blade.

teeth protruding above the chamfered edge. A small G-cramp is used at each end to hold the two sections securely to the blade for sharpening. The teeth themselves are sharpened straight across with a normal triangular saw file.

THE CIRCULAR SAW

The circular saw will give a perfectly straight cut and so is excellent for ripping down timber, although it is limited to the thickness of wood it can cope with. It comes in two basic forms: the hand-held or skill saw, and the bench or table saw. The former is ideal for cutting large sheets of manufactured board in a small workshop, but the bench saw is much better and safer for smaller pieces.

The portable circular saw or skill saw is regarded as a site tool and is useful for cutting large sheet material in any circumstance. It must be remembered that the blade cuts upwards and will tend to splinter the top surface and so it is always best to mark work out on the underside. The saw is used with the fence for accurate cutting but may also be used freehand. Make sure that the wood being cut is well supported and cramped in place so that both of your hands are available to hold the saw.

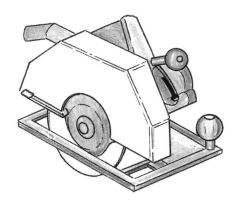

Hand-held circular saw.

THE TABLE SAW

This is the saw that we tend to think of as the standard circular saw. The blade projects up through the work table and can be raised or lowered, as required. The wood is fed into the blade while it is being held against a fence, and a push feed stick should be used to pass the end of smaller pieces of work between the fence and the blade. The height of the blade above the table is adjustable which means that rebating and grooving may be performed.

Every saw should be supplied with a crown guard to keep the hands clear of the blade, and a riving knife which is in line with the blade and enters the cut just made by it. The function of the riving knife is to prevent the timber from closing together after it is cut and thereby gripping the blade. If this were to happen the timber would be thrown back towards the operator with considerable force. When grooving, or for any operation where the riving knife has to be removed, a tunnel guard should be fitted as shown. The circular saw should be treated with great respect and maintained properly; more accidents occur with this type of saw than with any other piece of woodworking equipment. Never stand directly behind the blade in case the work is thrown back; always wear safety glasses or goggles; and keep the work area free from clutter.

To adjust the fence for ripping, the distance between its face and the top of the tooth that is set towards the fence is measured with a rule. The saw should always be turned off at the power supply before any operation is carried out involving contact with the blade. When the fence has been adjusted with the rule, a test piece of wood should be cut and the size of the cut timber measured to make sure that it is of the required size. It is not necessary to cut an entire length of wood for this purpose, a small cut in one end will be sufficient.

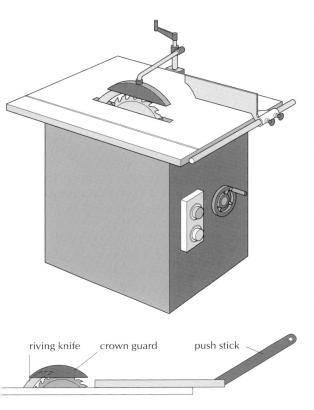

riving knife   crown guard   push stick

The table saw.

If the size needs to be adjusted this may be done with the fine adjustment control on the saw and the test piece cut again; it is not necessary to use the rule a second time. Further adjustments are made and checked until the desired dimension is achieved. The blade must be adjusted so that its height is just above that of the wood being cut and the crown guard should be set so that the gap between it and the work is no more than 12mm (½in).

Cross-Cutting

The saw will be supplied with a mitre fence which is used for cutting the ends of timber to size. The fence is adjustable and can be used for cutting mitres as well as square ends. The usual practice when squaring tim-ber off to length is to cut one end square and then measure and mark the other from this before cutting it off. Because with cross-cutting the lengths of timber are often much longer than the saw table alone will support, a trestle or some other form of sup-port should be used to help to support the timber being cut. Whatever support is used it must have a batten or other piece of wood which is chamfered at the top and fixed to the top surface at the same height as the saw table. The chamfering is done to reduce to a minimum the amount of drag exerted on the end of the wood. It is a good idea to keep the top chamfered edge of the batten waxed to provide 'slip' over the surface.

When cutting mitres or square ends it will be found that the wood will splinter where the blade exits. This is best over-come by fixing a wooden fence to the face of the one supplied and cutting the end after it has been adjusted to the desired angle. This will mean that the back of the wood is supported right up to the blade.

RADIAL ARM SAW

The radial arm saw is a huge asset to any small workshop. It may be used for ripping, cross-cutting, rebating, mitring and mould-ing. It is essentially an over-table circular saw attached to an adjustable arm, enabling the blade to be rotated to almost any position. The biggest difference that you will experi-ence between a conventional circular and a radial arm saw is in cross-cutting. When cross-cutting on a conventional saw the wood has to be fed into the blade and some resistance can be felt, whereas with the radial arm saw the operator needs to hold the blade back to some extent. In a large and well-equipped workshop the radial arm saw would be kept for cross-cutting and mitring but in the smaller workshop it may be necessary to use it for ripping. Ripping down timber with a radial arm saw should be regarded as a potentially dangerous

143

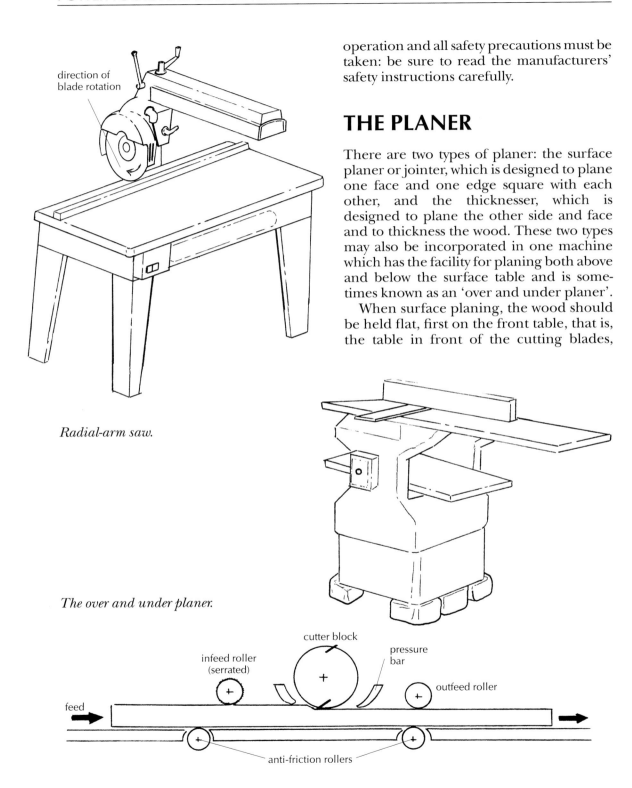

operation and all safety precautions must be taken: be sure to read the manufacturers' safety instructions carefully.

THE PLANER

There are two types of planer: the surface planer or jointer, which is designed to plane one face and one edge square with each other, and the thicknesser, which is designed to plane the other side and face and to thickness the wood. These two types may also be incorporated in one machine which has the facility for planing both above and below the surface table and is sometimes known as an 'over and under planer'.

When surface planing, the wood should be held flat, first on the front table, that is, the table in front of the cutting blades,

Radial-arm saw.

The over and under planer.

In operation, downward pressure must be applied to the back table as soon as possible.

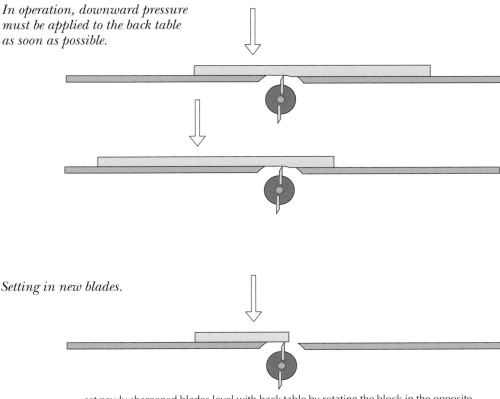

Setting in new blades.

set newly sharpened blades level with back table by rotating the block in the opposite direction to which it turns in operation so that they knock against a hardwood block; check both ends of the blade

and, as the work progresses past the blades, the hands should be used to keep the wood flat on the back table as quickly as possible. Once the face has been planed flat, it may be held against the planers fence and the edge planed square to it. With a thicknesser the wood may then be passed underneath on another table and planed to required thickness.

One of the main difficulties experienced with planers is in setting newly sharpened blades in place. It is necessary for the accurate operation of the machine for both blades to be exactly parallel with each other and at the same height as the back table. The cutters are secured in the cutter block with studs and adjustment may be a long and

tricky job. First secure the blades in place with the outer studs only, tightening them just enough to hold the blade in place. Hold a piece of flat, prepared hardwood on the back table so that it overlaps the cutter block to one side. Rotate the cutter block in the opposite direction to which it would turn in operation, so that the blades knock against the hardwood block. Repeat this operation on the other side, tighten the studs a little more and repeat the process until both blades are parallel and only just touch the hardwood block. Fully tighten all the studs.

The thickness of cut is controlled by altering the height of the front table *only*. The height of the back table is altered only when setting in new blades.

— 17 —

Finishing

PREPARATION

The degree to which wood has to be prepared before finishing depends upon the finish required. Garden sheds, fences and even summer houses may need no more preparation than the rounding off of vulnerable corners if they are to be treated with only wood preserver or creosote. On the other hand, any item which is to be painted will need to be sanded down before the paint is applied, and even sanded between coats for a really good finish. Furniture and similar items which are to be polished will need a great deal of preparation if an acceptable finish is to be obtained. Unlike paint, polishes and lacquers will tend to highlight blemishes rather than cover them up.

To prepare a piece of newly constructed furniture for finishing the first step after cleaning it up with the smoothing plane and cabinet scrape is to sand all areas thoroughly in the direction of the grain. Care must be taken in those places where rails join with differing grain directions not to sand over the edge on to an area of differing grain as this will cause scratching and show up when the piece is polished. Start with a medium grit paper, then a fine one and finish with flour paper. On curved or rounded areas the paper may be held in the hand, but on flat surfaces it is best to wrap the paper around a cork sanding block. The use of a block means that pressure can be applied more evenly over the area and you are less likely to round off corners that need to be kept sharp.

Once the initial sanding is complete, the grain will have to be raised and the raised grain sanded down. This is done because otherwise the grain will rise when stain is applied, and there is a possibility that you will sand through the stain when rubbing this down causing an unsightly fleck. Raising the grain is done by applying hot water to the surface of the work and drying it with a hair dryer. The water must not be allowed to become cold before the drying because this may cause black marks to form with some woods. On some I have found that the grain will rise again on a second application of hot water, and it is worthwhile repeating the operation. Dust the work thoroughly and check for any scratches or blemishes which may have been missed; extra time spent in preparation can save headaches later.

Finally, all sanding, even if done with a machine sander with a dust bag, will put dust in the air, so always wear a dust mask.

STOPPERS AND FILLERS

Sometimes, even when the greatest care has been taken throughout the work, stopper will be required, as is often the case with knotty woods or burr veneers. Before resorting to stopper, however, consider whether there are any other alternatives, such as letting in a piece of wood.

The main types of stopper available are described below.

PLASTIC WOOD

This stopper is really only suitable for inferior or painted work as it does not take stain. Its advantages are that it dries quickly and can be purchased in a tube. The stopper is applied with a putty knife or piece of stick and must be left slightly proud of the surface and then sanded level when dry.

BRUMMER STOPPER

Brummer is available in both interior and exterior grades and comes in a variety of colours which may be mixed together for colour matching. The colour tends to lighten on drying and so it is best to try it on a piece of waste timber first to check the dry colour. Brummer is applied with a putty or pallet knife and must be left proud of the surface and then sanded level when dry.

SHELLAC FILLER STICKS

These hard shellac sticks come in a variety of colours and are melted into the crack or defect with a hot tool such as a soldering iron. These too must be left proud of the surface and sanded level after drying.

POLISHER'S PUTTY

It is possible to make a quick drying putty by mixing together button polish or shellac with whiting and dry pigments. Mix a little whiting with the pigments and then add the button polish and mix to a soft paste; make slightly more than you will require in order first to allow a little to dry in order to test the colour, this will lighten considerably on drying. Apply the mixture immediately to the work because it will dry very quickly and leave proud of the surface to be sanded level when it is dry.

WAX FILLER STICKS

These can be purchased in a wide range of colours; they become soft and pliable when warm, allowing them to be mixed together. To use, they are warmed and kneaded between the fingers and then pressed into the crack with a shaped hardwood stick and rubbed down flush with the surface. The rubbing down is first done using the stick to remove the bulk of the excess of stopper; the finishing is done with a waxy rag until the stopper is flush with the surface. Wax stopper is generally used after the polishing process is finished; but it is possible to use it under shellac if the first coats are applied with a rubber.

GRAIN FILLER

Grain fillers are used to clog or choke the grain so that less polish will be required. They also contain colour and so great care is needed in their selection for any particular job. They are rubbed over the surface, across the grain and allowed to partially dry before having the excess wiped off. Knowing how long to leave the filler on the surface before the wiping off is the secret: too long and it is difficult to remove unless softened, too soon and it will be wiped out of the grain, defeating the object of its use. The answer is to try some on another piece of wood and wipe off a little of it at periodically; when the time is right, wipe off the work in hand.

STAINING

There are several types of wood stain on the market: oil stains which are soluble in petroleum spirit; spirit stains which are soluble in methylated spirits; and water stain which is soluble in water. Bichromate of potash (potassium dichromate) is useful for colouring both mahogany and oak; although it is a waterborne chemical rather than a true wood stain, it is used in the same way as a water stain.

All wood stains are applied with a brush, the surface being thoroughly covered and particular attention being paid to corners and mouldings. Some oily woods, or old furniture which has been stripped with paint remover, may need the stain to be rubbed on lightly with 0000 grade wire wool to help it to penetrate the surface.

The most important part of staining comes in wiping away the excess of stain. This is done with a clean, absorbent cloth, in the direction of the grain wherever possible. Wipe fairly hard to make sure that all the excess is removed and no streaks remain. End grain will naturally take stain quicker and deeper than long grain, and appear darker, therefore make sure that all end grain has been treated with hot water at least twice. One good tip is to apply a little solvent to the end grain first in order to cut down the absorption. With very open end grain it is even possible to apply a coat of transparent sealer and then sand it back to the bare wood before staining. It is important that the stain is completely dry before any finish is applied.

OIL STAIN

These stains have a white spirit or white spirit and naphtha base and are readily available from DIY shops in a variety of colours. The colours may be mixed together and in practice it is better to buy more than one colour and mix rather than to rely on only one. The mahogany, for example, tends to be a strong red and may well benefit from being mixed with some light oak to give a more natural colour.

Apply the stain with a rag or brush and wipe off the excess with a dry cloth in the direction of the grain. Because these stains are white spirit-based, any finish, such as varnish, which is also similarly based will tend to move the stain and will need to have a coat of shellac applied first as a sealer.

SPIRIT STAINS

These are purchased in powder form and are mixed with methylated spirits. Spirit stains dry quickly and a wet edge has to be maintained throughout their application if streaking is to be avoided. This makes them difficult to apply to complicated structures, such as bookcases, where there may be many shelves because overlapping is difficult to avoid. When the stain is dry it needs to be fixed with a coat of shellac.

WATER STAINS

Water stains come in ready mixed or powder form. The powders are best mixed in hot, or at least warm, water and allowed to cool before use. They are applied with a brush and wiped off evenly in the direction of the grain with a dry cloth. Sometimes, when the piece being stained has been previously polished and stripped for repolishing, the stain needs to be applied with 0000 wire wool. This will help it to penetrate the waxy finish which may be left by some strippers. When wiping off the excess of stain, which must be done in the direction of the grain, care must be taken not to leave any streaks. The drying time is dependent on the room temperature but may be hastened with a hair dryer.

VARNISH STAINS

These coloured varnishes are not suitable for fine cabinetwork, but the external grades are ideal for doors and windows. They are available in a variety of colours in gloss, satin and matt finish. Work the varnish into the grain and the corners of the work, keeping a wet edge and finish with an almost dry brush in the direction of the grain.

HOLDING WORK FOR POLISHING

If a cabinet is being polished after it has been constructed it may simply be stood on wooden blocks to keep it off the floor. Sometimes, however, it may be beneficial to polish components before their assembly. Panels, for instance, need to be free to move in their frame and, if stained and polished after being assembled, would show a light area where the panel shrinks. Therefore they are best polished first, likewise doors, bureau falls and other items which are attached by hinges. Some method of holding these components during polishing will be needed. Simply to lay them on the bench is not good enough; they may easily be damaged and thus it is best to lift the work off the bench by placing it on battens. In this way the edges may be polished without the danger of the brush's becoming contaminated by contact with the bench top. If both sides of a component are to be polished, the top edges of the batten may be planed to a sharp edge so that only a very small amount is in contact with the work, reducing the risk of damage to the soft polish. Allow enough time for the polish to dry before turning the panel over.

NON-REVERSIBLE FINISHES

Most of the finishes that you will buy, such as polyurethane and varnishes, are non-reversible, that is to say, that once they have dried they cannot be softened by application of their solvent.

One or two coats of these finishes with a brush are normally enough, but this must be done in a warm, dust-free environment. It is usually best, in a small workshop, first to use a vacuum cleaner and then to it leave for an hour or so for any remaining dust to settle before commencing to apply the finish. Make sure that the whole surface is well covered, but avoid too much brushing because this causes aeration and a poor result in a quick-drying finish. Try to flood the finish on to the surface and to brush lightly in the direction of the grain, beginning in the centre and working out to the edges.

These finishes can normally have a second coat within four hours, but be sure to read the manufacturer's instructions. The second coat will need to be left for several

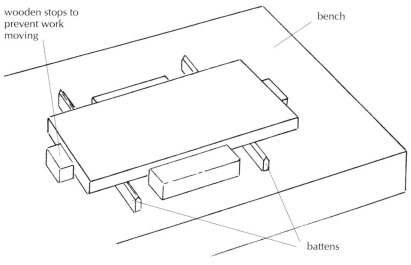

Panel held in place for polishing.

days to harden rather than just to dry. Once hard, it can be brought to a high gloss by rubbing, first with a fine wet and dry paper, used wet to remove any brush marks, and then with a burnishing cream, such as those used for car-body work. If a satin finish is required, the surface can be rubbed down with 0000 wire wool and then waxed.

TECHNIQUES AND MATERIALS

THE CARE OF BRUSHES AND MOPS

One of the most common and infuriating problems associated with any finish requiring the use of a brush or polishing mop is loose hairs getting on to the newly polished surface. New brushes especially seem to shed hairs as if they had a moulting season. This may be largely overcome by the preparation of the brush.

The brush or mop must be suspended in shellac for at least two days before use. This can be accomplished by driving a small wire nail or pin into the side of the brush and bending its end over slightly so that it can be hung on the inside of a jar without its resting on the hairs. The brush must be deep enough in the shellac so that the hairs are entirely covered, up past that section of the brush where they are secured. Over this period shellac will work its way into the uppermost regions of the bristles, after which the brush should be removed. Wipe the excess from the brush and allow it to dry until the shellac is quite hard, which should take several days. The brush should then be suspended in methylated spirits in the same way as it was in the shellac, but this time only to the top of the *exposed* bristles. After this procedure the bristles should be well secured in place and not give a problem with shedding hairs.

Although this process takes several days I recommend it for all new brushes.

Brushes used for applying paint and non-reversible finishes should be cleaned after each use with the appropriate solvent. Polishing mops that are used with shellac or button polish may be left suspended in the polish more or less permanently, provided that the hairs do not reach the bottom of the jar.

WAX FINISH

Beeswax is the basis of furniture wax and there are several varieties on the market, or you can make your own by putting some shredded beeswax in a pan with turpentine and then placing the pan in hot water to dissolve the wax, stirring all the while. It is best to apply the wax when it is fairly soft and allow it to dry for a while before buffing up. This will have to be done several times to obtain a good result, but the process can be speeded up by applying one or two coats of shellac or button polish to the bare wood before the waxing is done.

FRENCH POLISH

French polish, button polish and garnet polish are all made from shellac, which is the secretion of the lac beetle. Garnet polish is dark brown in colour; button polish is deep orange and French polish is amber. Shellac can also be bleached to produce white or transparent polish for use on very light woods. All these polishes may be used in the same way and applied with a polishing mop or a rubber.

Application by Mop
The polishing mop is made of either bear, zorrino or squirrel hair and comes in sizes ranging from a small No.4 to a large No.14, but a No.8 or 10 is capable of handling most jobs. The mop is used to apply polish to areas difficult to cover with a pad, such as

the inside of a cabinet where it would be difficult to get into the corners. It is also used when just one or two coats are required for sealing stain or under a wax finish.

To use it, charge the mop with polish and wipe it on the side of the jar so that it is not too full; polish should run out of the mop only when it is in contact with the work. Start at the back edge and towards but not at one end, work backwards and forwards from end to end, gradually working towards the front edge until the mop is nearly dry. Recharge the mop with polish and repeat. Do not start exactly at the wet edge but a mop's width away, work back towards the wet edge at first and then away from it until the mop is almost empty. Repeat these actions until the near side is reached. Make sure that the edges of the work are covered and that any runs underneath are wiped with the finger to spread them out. The polishing mop will have to be used on any mouldings or carving, but once again be careful not to overcharge the mop with polish so as to avoid runs and pooling.

Application with a Rubber
The rubber is made of non-surgical cotton wool covered with clean cotton rag. The cotton wool will keep its shape better if placed inside the leg of an old pair of tights, this also helps to stop pieces of wool from getting on to the work. To start, the pad is charged with polish which has been slightly thinned with methylated spirits. To load the rubber, remove the cotton rag and pour a quantity of polish on to the cotton wool. Try to distribute the polish evenly over the face of the rubber, and then cover with the cotton rag. As the rubber is placed on the work, polish will be squeezed out on to the surface. The rubber must be kept moving over the surface in all directions across the grain, with the grain and in figure-of-eight movements; at no time should the rubber be stationary on the work.

When the rubber is first filled it may be necessary to go over the surface once; leave it for a moment or two and then go over it again However, after a while it should be possible to keep going over the surface continually, without lifting the pad off. The idea at this stage, known as 'fadding', is to get as much polish on the surface and into the grain as possible. The pad should move easily over the surface, applying a little polish as it goes, without its feeling 'sticky'. If the pad does begin to feel sticky, move the covering rag so that a new, clean area presents itself to the work. After a while it will be necessary to leave the work to harden a little, possibly overnight, and start the next day by sanding the surface with a fine paper. The pad can be kept in an airtight jar to prevent its drying out. As the work progresses and the grain becomes fuller, thinner and thinner polish is used. Keep moving to a clean area of rag if you feel any drag or stickiness. At this stage, known as 'bodying-up', the continual movement of the pad is burnishing as well as applying more polish. Continue in this way until the grain is completely filled and you have a good, shiny surface. If the pad feels sticky even with a new piece of rag, white polishing oil may be used as a lubricant, by placing a little on the palm of the hand and wiping the edge of the pad in it. Do not use too much oil as it will later have to be removed.

The final stage is known as 'stiffing' and a completely new pad should be made. This is charged with one-third polish and two-thirds methylated spirits, but only a very small amount of polish is used. This time the rubber is used in line with the grain only from end to end, each stroke overlapping and coming off the work at each end. Care must be taken when the rubber is placed back on the work each time: the rubber must be moving as it touches the surface of the work. This process will gradually remove any oil and when this is achieved the rubber should have a little stiffness; this is an indication that the work is finished.

Spiriting-Off

Spiriting-off is used to impart an extra shine to the surface and to remove any oil remaining after stiffing. A completely new rubber is made and charged with a small amount of pure methylated spirits. Once this is done, the new pad is placed in an air-tight jar to allow the spirit to permeate it. Go over the work with this new pad in the same way as before and this will gradually lift off any oil that was left and also impart a fine high-gloss finish to the work.

French polish may take as much as three months to harden fully, depending on the amount of polish used and the environment it is in. When fully hardened French polish is a good, durable finish although it is not suitable for dining or coffee table-tops which may be subjected to heat or spirits.

OIL FINISH

Oil is possibly the most heat- and stain-resistant of all the finishes. Linseed oil is the traditional treatment for cricket bats and outdoor furniture, but this takes a long time to dry and today there are alternatives available, the best of which are tung oil or Liberon finishing oil, both of which dry much more quickly.

The oil is applied to bare wood with a rag, working the oil into the grain by going at first across it and then finishing in line with the grain. Elbow grease is required in the application of oil and the rubbing in should continue until all the oil has been rubbed in. The oil must now be allowed to dry and this may take as long as two days; but if you are using a commercial product then be sure to read the instructions on the container. When the oil is dry it should be rubbed down with fine wire wool and the surface then dusted with a rag, dampened with a little water or methylated spirits. The process is repeated until the desired finish is obtained. It is possible to impart a little extra shine to the surface when finished by rubbing down with 0000 wire wool and waxing.

It is important to note that oils that contain drying agents dry by oxidation, which means that any rag that has been used for oiling could spontaneously combust. It is essential that any such rags are either washed after use in hot, soapy water or disposed of in a sealed container.

Glossary of Woodworking Terms

Woodwork is a huge subject and not all the terms listed here have been used in the book, but a knowledge of them is likely to prove useful.

Abutment: a support resisting horizontal thrust; the pier from which an arch springs

Adze: a carpenter's tool used for squaring logs and levelling surfaces

Angle brace: a tie to strengthen the angle of framing

Angle joint: any joint that joins timbers that are not in a straight line

Annual rings: the concentric annual growth rings of a tree

Architrave: ornamental moulding around a door, window or niche

Auger: a twist bit for drilling holes

Back flap: a hinge for use on doors, etc

Back saw: any saw that has a stiffening strip of steel or brass along its back, such as a tenon saw

Ball catch: a plate carrying a steel ball let into the edge of a swing door to secure it in place when closed

Balusters: small, vertical pillars supporting a handrail

Balustrade: a row of balusters with the base and rail forming a protective enclosure to a balcony or stairs

Bandings: narrow inlays in cabinetwork

Bas-relief: low relief; carving projecting only slightly above the surface of the material of which it is a part

Bench hook: used for steadying small pieces of wood for cutting on the bench

Bench stop: an adjustable projection at the end of a bench against which wood is planed

Bits: the drills used in a hand or wheel brace as in twist bit

Blade: the metal part of a combined wood and metal tool such as a try-square

Bodger: the turner of chair legs, etc. in woodcraft

Bolection (balection) moulding: a rebated panel moulding, the face of which stands above the face of the framing

Bombe: an arched or convex surface in cabinetmaking

Boss: a carved block covering the joint between cross-timbers or the end of a beam

Boule-work: a marquetry veneer of brass and tortoiseshell

Bracket: a support projecting from a vertical surface

Brad: a nail cut or stamped from sheet material

Buffet: a sideboard or small cupboard for the dining room

Burr: abnormal growth on a tree from which decorative veneers can be cut

Button: a small piece of wood secured with a single screw so that it is free to turn; used as a door closure or to hold the tops on tables

Cabriole: applied to uprights, such as legs, where the upper part swells outwards and the lower part inwards

Cambium: the wood forming part of the living tree just under the bark

Cant: an external, splayed angle

Cantilever: a beam supported at one end only

Carborundum: silicon carbide, made by heating coke with sand in a furnace; used for oilstones and as an abrasive

Cartouche: a carved tablet in the form of a scroll used for an inscription

Carvel: applied to the side planking of a boat where the planks present a flush surface

Casement: a hinged or pivoted sash

Caul: a wooden, heated press used in veneering to keep the veneer in place until the glue is dry

Caulk: to fill or stop an open joint to make it watertight

Chase: to cut a groove or channel in metal or wood

Cheval: a long, swivelled mirror

Chevron: a zigzag moulding or inlay

Chippendale (Thomas): eighteenth-century English cabinet maker

Chops: a frame for clamping the edge of a saw while sharpening it

Chord: any straight line across a circle that terminates with each end at the circumference

Clearance: a space between two surfaces to prevent contact

Cleft: applied to timber that is split instead of sawn

Clinch: turning over the projecting point of a nail to prevent its withdrawal

Clinker: applied to the side planking of a boat where the planks overlap

Clout nail: a short nail with a large, flat head for fixing felt and cord

Concentric: applied to circles or arcs struck from the same centre but having different radii

Console: a large, ornamental bracket

Console table: a narrow table against the pier of a wall supported on a decorative bracket

Cooper: a craftsman who makes and repairs casks and barrels

Cornice: a large, projecting moulding at the top of a piece of furniture or at the junction of a wall and ceiling

Cove or coving: a hollow or concave moulding

Crossbanding: a veneered banding around the edge of a top or panel in which the grain is at right angles to the main work

Crown: the highest point of an arch or other ornamental feature

Crown cut: sawn tangentially to a tree's annual rings

Curl: decorative grain in wood cut from the junction of a branch with the trunk

Dado: the lower part of a room when lined or painted separately

Davenport: a small writing desk with a sloping top and drawers usually down one side

Dog: an iron fastening for timber consisting of a length of iron bent over at right angles and pointed at each end

Donkey: a wooden frame used as a stool when cutting veneers for marquetry

Door check: a device for controlling the closing of a door

Dormer: a window with vertical casements in a sloping roof

Dressed: applied to timber that is planed on one or more sides

Dumb waiter: a small lift for conveying food or crockery

Dust boards: the horizontal panels between drawers

Ebonize: to stain or dye wood to resemble ebony

Escutcheon: an ornamental plate covering a keyhole, or an armorial shield

False tenon: a hardwood tenon that is inserted into a mortise in both pieces being joined and not formed from either

Fanlight: originally applied to the semicircular sash with radiating bars over a door but now applied to any shape of window over the transom of a door

Featheredge: applied to boards that taper in thickness

Ferrule: a metal ring around a handle or the like to prevent its splitting

Festoon: a carved ornament in the shape of a garland suspended from its two ends

Fielded panel: a raised panel with a large flat surface

Fillet: small strips of wood or shelf supports

Finial: an ornamental projection at the top or apex of a canopy, gable or newel

Firsts: term used in the grading of timber to denote the best quality

Flap: that part of a tabletop that can be raised or lowered

Flitch: a log prepared for conversion to veneers, or the pile of veneers themselves after conversion

Flogging: levelling the joints of floorboards

Floor dog: a cramp used for floorboards

Flourpaper: a very fine abrasive paper

Flutes: concave grooves as in a pillar or column

Fly leaf: a hinged leaf to a table

Fly rail: a rail that is drawn or swung out to support a leaf

French doors: a pair of large sashes, hinged and used as doors

Frieze: the top part of an internal wall between the picture rail and the cornice

Fuming: darkening oak with ammonia

Gesso: a plaster made from whiting and glue size used as a base for painted decoration

Godroon: carved ornament in the form of a cable or bead

Green: applied to unseasoned wood

Hasp: a hinged and slotted plate that fits over a staple to be locked in place with a padlock

Hepplewhite (George): eighteenth-century English cabinet maker

Herringbone: an obliquely alternating pattern giving a zigzag effect arising from the grain of timber laid in a parallel arrangement

Hook: amount the iron projects from the base of a plane

Jacobean: English style of the early seventeenth century

Jamb: vertical piece forming the side of a doorway or window

Japanned: applied to fittings that are covered with a hard black varnish for protection

Kerf: the groove cut by a saw

Knuckle: that part of a hinge that contains the pin or pivot

Knuckle joint: a hinge-type of joint used for fly rails

Lacquer: varnish used on metals to prevent their tarnishing

Lathe: machine for turning wood

Lever lock: a lock in which several levers are lifted by the key to shoot the bolt

Limed oak: a finish obtained by rubbing the wood with a paste of chloride of lime (bleaching powder); other materials are now available to give the same effect

Linings: the sides, backs and bottoms of drawers

Lintel: a horizontal beam across an opening

Lopers: slides to support a table leaf or bureau fall

Louver/louvre: inclined slats forming a shutter or ventilator

Lozenge: small diamond- or rhomboid-shaped carving

Lumber: American term for converted timber

Margin: the projection of a stair string above the nosing line

Mason's mitre: a mitre of a moulding that is actually butt jointed and carved in the solid to give the appearance of being mitred

MDF: medium-density fibre board

Medullary rays: radial rays in the cross-section of a tree trunk that are vertical sheets of tissue formed across the growth rings

Mezzanine: a low storey between the levels of two main floors

Nest: applied to a set of similar objects usually diminishing in size, such as a nest of tables

Niche: a small recess in a wall for a statue or ornament

Oblique: not at right angles, perpendicular or parallel to a given reference point

Obtuse: applied to angles greater than 90 degrees

Ogee: a moulding consisting of one concave and one convex shallow curve

Oriel: a bay window usually semipolygonal in shape

Parquet: surfaces formed from small pieces of wood arranged in geometrical designs

Paterae: circular or elliptical ornamentation on friezes and furniture

Pediment: ornamental head to a doorway or other opening

Pembroke: a small table with flaps on either side

Pendent: ornamental finish to the bottom of a suspended post or newel

Pier: a support of brick, stone or concrete

Pier glass: a long, narrow mirror fixed on a wall between two windows

Pier table: one supporting a pier or wall mirror

Pigeon-hole: a small space in a desk or other fitment for storing papers

Plucked up: term used when the grain has been torn up through careless use of the plane

Poker-work: designs made on wood with a red-hot needle or poker; more properly pyrography

Pommel: a spherical ornament

Quirk: a narrow, flat groove in a moulding

Rafter: roof timber running from ridge to wall plate

Raised panel: a panel that is thicker in the middle than at the edges

Rasp: like a rough file, but with separate teeth instead of furrows

Sabot: metal fitting at the end of a leg

Saw chops: any appliance for holding a saw while it is being sharpened

Scantlings: wood of small size and varied dimensions left over after conversion

Sconce: a bracket carrying a light or reflector

Second fixing: applied to joinery that is fitted after plastering

Shingles: wooden tiles used for covering roofs and exterior walls

Shuttering: wooden formwork used for retaining concrete until it is dry

Silver grain: figure produced by the medullary rays (q.v.) in quarter-sawn timber such as oak

Slip feather: a thin slip of wood or veneer used to strengthen a mitre joint

Squab: a loose cushion for a couch or chair

Stair rod: a wood or metal rod to secure a carpet to stairs

Stile: an upright member in panelling or framing

Tooling: simple, shallow carving or the gold-leaf designs on leather inserts

Tracery: mullions and bars arranged in geometrical patterns

Tudor: English style of the sixteenth century

Vitrine: a display cabinet with daylight background

Wainscoting: wall panelling of wood especially up to dado height

William and Mary: English style of the late seventeenth century

Windsor chair: a wooden chair with a hoop-shaped back filled with turned spindles

Glossary of Woods

SOFTWOODS

Cedar: pale brown in colour with a strong fragrance, true cedar comes from Morocco and should not be confused with the red cedar of the United States; the latter reaches considerable dimensions and is the one used for pencil making

Douglas fir: known also as Columbian or Oregon pine; it has a light reddish-brown heartwood with much paler sapwood; Douglas fir is one of North America's most important construction timbers

Parana pine: so called because it grows chiefly in the Brazilian state of Parana but it is also to be found in Paraguay and northern Argentina; brown heartwood with occasional red streaks, it is otherwise pale; this wood is almost knot-free and is used for staircases and in cabinet making

Pitch pine: yellow to red-brown in colour and very resinous, this wood was much used by the Victorians for staircases, church pews and school fittings

Scots pine: grows from Spain to Siberia; the slower growing trees from the north have closely spaced growth rings and a fine texture that make them suitable for furniture

Spruce: white in colour, this makes it an ideal wood for the paper industry; spruce is not very durable and is little used in woodwork except for the Sitka spruce that is used in the manufacture of gliders

Yew: a strong, resilient wood, yew has a reddish-brown heartwood with irregular growth rings; mostly used today as a veneer or for small ornamental turnings

HARDWOODS

African blackwood: very dense and black, this is the wood of oboes and clarinets

Abura: from West Africa, this timber has no growth rings and is a uniform yellow-brown or pinkish-beige in colour; abura is much used today for drawer linings and for other purposes where a stable wood is required

Afrormosia: from West Africa, this wood is yellow-brown when fresh but goes dark with age; afrormosia resembles teak and is often used as a substitute for it

Apple: an even texture with a slight pinkish tinge make this an attractive wood that lends itself to delicate carving and inlay work

Ash (American): American ash comes in three different species – white ash, green ash and black ash; white and green ash are grey-brown, sometimes with a red tint; black ash is darker in colour and lighter in weight; ash is used in cabinet making and also for the handles of spades and other tools

Ash (European): a pale but attractive timber used for furniture and tool handles, it also bends well and is often used for boat frames and bentwood furniture

Beech: beech varies in colour from off-white to light brown, but is often steamed which gives it a pinkish tinge; the wood is used mostly in the furniture industry because it turns and bends well and may be stained to almost any colour; beech is the wood that has traditionally been used to support upholstery because it grips the tacks better than any other

Birch: pale brown or whitish in colour, birch is usually straight-grained even though it usually has a large number of knots

Box: pale yellow in colour with a very fine grain, box is limited in size and is most often used for inlay or small decorative items

Cherry: light brown with a pink tinge when new, this wood matures to a deep reddish-brown; cherry is used for high-quality furniture and decorative inlays

Ebony: usually thought of as jet black, many planks are valued for their lighter streaks; ebony is hard and difficult to work and is used mostly for inlay work or the fingerboards of musical instruments

Elm: English elm is dull brown in colour with strong figure; it is moderately tough and an excellent shock absorber; traditionally used for structural work, piling, furniture and coffins

Hickory: white to yellow-brown in colour with darker striations; the wood is hard and strong but not durable; used for items that have to withstand violent shock such as baseball bats, drumsticks and hammers

Lime: yellowish in colour, lime has a fine, close grain and is often used for turning and carving

Mahogany (African): orange-brown in colour, with a stripy figure on quarter-sawn surfaces

Mahogany (American): there are many different types of mahogany and they are usually distinguished by their place of origin: Cuban, Honduras or Brazil, for instance, and described as plain or figured. They are generally reddish brown in colour and used for cabinet work, superior joinery and veneers

Maple: faint brownish-white in colour, hard and compact with a fine lustrous grain, maple is used for furniture and superior joinery; the figured woods, especially bird's eye, are generally used for decorative veneers

Oak (American): light to medium brown with a yellowish tinge, it is used in much the same ways as European oak; acid in oak will corrode iron, lead and other reactive metals

Oak (European): golden brown in colour, oak is synonymous with strength and durability and has been used for flooring, boat-building, construction work and furniture

Obeche: this varies in appearance from light coffee-coloured to almost white; obeche is suitable for internal joinery or furniture parts where strength is not required

Padauk: purple-brown in colour, padauk is a very hard and durable wood used for flooring and other areas that require resistance to wear; it may be purchased as a veneer

Pear: rosy-pink in colour with a delicate, regular texture, pear is mostly used for small decorative items

Rosewood: a dark wood with a purplish hue and fine black streaks, it gets its name from its rose-like fragrance; rosewood is used for furniture, pianos and fine decorative items

Sapele: sapele is a rich golden or reddish-brown and used as a substitute for mahogany

Teak: golden brown at first, it becomes darker and reddish in time; strong, durable and hard-wearing, teak is used for boat-building, flooring and furniture, especially for gardens

Walnut: light brown in colour with dark streaks that give it a distinctive grain, walnut was widely used for panelling and furniture; a strong and lightweight wood, it is easy to work and polishes well.

Index